Horace Waters

Sabbath-School Bell

Number 2

Horace Waters

Sabbath-School Bell
Number 2

ISBN/EAN: 9783337772543

Printed in Europe, USA, Canada, Australia, Japan

Cover: Foto ©Lupo / pixelio.de

More available books at **www.hansebooks.com**

[Price 15 Cents.]

A Superior

SABBATH SCHOOL

Collection of

CHOICE TUNES, NEWLY ARRANGED AND COMPOSED, AND A LARGE NUM-
BER OF EXCELLENT HYMNS.

WRITTEN EXPRESSLY FOR THIS WORK, WHICH ARE WELL ADAPTED FOR SUNDAY SCHOOLS, REVIVAL MEETINGS, ANNI-
VERSARIES, CHRISTMAS FESTIVALS, CONCERTS, PIC-NICS, TEMPERANCE MEETINGS, BOYS' AND GIRLS'
MEETINGS, EXCURSIONS, ETC., ETC., CAREFULLY AND SIMPLY ARRANGED AS SOLOS, DUETS,
QUARTETS, SEMI-CHORUSES, AND CHORUSES, AND FOR PIANO OR MELODEON.

EDITED BY HORACE WATERS,

Author of Sabbath School Bell No. 1, Anniversary and Sunday School Music Books Nos. 1, 2, 3, 4, 5, 6,
and 7, and Revival Melodies.

NEW YORK:

PUBLISHED BY HORACE WATERS, No. 333 BROADWAY.

PREFACE.

THIS little book, like its predecessor, is designed for the use of children. It speaks, or rather, sings, for itself, and needs no introduction to those who understand and appreciate music. Should it fall under the notice of those who are jealous of original songs and tunes, or who look with suspicion on the new adaptation of old ones, the publisher would say to such, that all music is sacred, although it is sometimes, like the livery of heaven, used for profane purposes. Music is the language of heaven—it is the dialect of the angels; and if children or adults needed an excuse for pouring out their hearts and souls in strains of sacred harmony, we might refer them to the holy and beautiful example of the great and good men of all ages—the songs of the Patriarchs and Prophets, and the sweet strains of the holy choir about the Throne of God in Heaven. Moses is stern, bold, and original; his song a mere transcript of the scene in which he moved, but his language, though unadorned with metaphor, like the mountain on which he received the Commandments, is sublime and lofty. Deborah sang with spirit, as she rose from her seat on the hill-side, under the shadow of the palms. There is the ring of martial music in her song; but her hard words, that fall like hail upon the enemies of Israel, melt in tears of tenderness when she sees the mother of Sisera looking from the window. David is the great singer of the church: now his harp swells with grandeur and sublimity, until its chords shiver in the tempest of his passion; now he shudders over his own history, and his song sounds like the wail of a broken heart. His words are smiles and sighs, and tears. His lyrics are unrivalled in literature. Passing hastily over the example of the inspired men of the Bible, omitting even the names of many distinguished for their epic and lyric grandeur and harmony, we hasten to the highest authority that comes direct from heaven to earth—the song of the holy angels announcing the advent of the Saviour. What a scene to contemplate!—a choir of angels coming from the crystal walls and golden gates of Heaven. While the shepherds were watching their flocks, or studying the stars, suddenly a great glory breaks in beauty on the sky, blotting out the luster of the stars, and flooding the hemisphere with light. With this glorious effulgence comes the sweep of wings and the song of angels. "And lo! the angel of the Lord came upon them, and the glory of the Lord shone round about them: and they were sore afraid. And the angel said unto them, 'fear not; for behold! I bring you good tidings of great joy, which shall be to all people. For unto you is born, this day, in the city of David, a Saviour, which is Christ the Lord. And this shall

PREFACE.

be a sign unto you—ye shall find the babe wrapped in swadling clothes, lying in a manger.' And suddenly there was with the angel a multitude of the heavenly host, praising God and saying: 'Glory to God in the highest! and on earth peace, good will toward men." Children have the lesson of the angels—the song of the "multitude of the heavenly host,"—and every child should have a hymn in his heart; so that the song can break from the lips as naturally as the carol comes from the bird, when Nature spreads her note-book of flowers before it. Singing sweetens the temper, softens the voice, strengthens the lungs, is a rich source of entertainment to all who are virtuous and good. The songs of to-day may be the statutes of to-morrow. Music is the language of passion and emotion; it is beautiful thought crystalized into sound; and well becomes the hearts, and lips, and voices of children.

Among this music will be found many of the best and most stirring airs, united with sacred words, and invested with new associations. It is well known that many secular compositions possess unequaled excellence and power as music, and are especially adapted by their animation and embodiment of the true idea of music, to interest the young. In connection with the new sentiments they utter, their former associations will be forgotten, and their fire and spirit be secured for the inculcation of holier sentiments? Music, in itself, is never immoral or hurtful; on the contrary, it is essentially holy. The true home and source of music is Heaven; lost spirits may howl and curse, but never sing. And if connected with holy sentiments, its influence never fails to second and enforce truth, and every virtuous feeling.

This book is not only a song-book, but an educator; for while it interests the children, the solos, ducts, trios, and quartetts are so arranged that the choruses call for responses from parents, teachers, and all who may attend the meetings; thus kindling an enthusiasm generally for sacred music. And this is not only proper, but Scriptural. As in the multitude of the heavenly host, every angel joined the chorus—not one was silent; so in the songs of the Sabbath School or Concert, all should copy the example of these holy messengers, and sing; there should not be an exception:—old and young should join in the chorus. In the 136th Psalm we find the priest chanting, "Oh, give thanks unto the Lord, for he is good," and the people, or the congregation, responding, "for his mercy endureth for ever." "Oh, give thanks unto the God of gods," Chorus, "for his mercy endureth for ever," and so on to the close of this wonderful and beautiful psalm. The priest sang the solo, and the congregation replied with the chorus. It is like the ebbing and flowing of the tide:—now the wave sweeps from the shore to the sea; then the multitudinous

PREFACE.

billows break broad and deep upon the beach;—like deep calling unto deep. This arrangement of the music is a desideratum in the book, tending directly to educate the people, old and young, in the sacred science of harmonious sounds. All are invited to participate in these songs. While the Children sing, their friends and others are cordially and earnestly requested to join in the Chorus, so that all the people may unite in singing the songs of the Sabbath School children. And this corresponds with the ideas and practice of the greatest composers, and other masters of song. All the great productions of Handel, Haydn, Mozart, and others, bear a similar character of responsive alternation of parts, as solos, duets, trios, choruses, &c., and derive their principal element of power and attraction from this source. In a more simple manner, yet realizing the same principle, most of the pieces in this book have been arranged in this natural and efficient manner.

And this is not all. We thus sing the Gospel of glad tidings to the impenitent, melting the soul into sympathy by the tender pathos of pure sentiment. So wonderful is the power of song, it touches the chords that vibrate in the human breast, and thrills the heart with rapture, so that it often melts in contrition at the foot of the Cross; and vast multitudes are in this way converted to God: and we hope by the instrumentality of this book to sing a great multitude into the kingdom of Heaven.

This Volume, SABBATH SCHOOL BELL, No. 2, is entirely distinct from its predecessor, BELL, No. 1. The words and music are all different, and, in our judgment, better adapted to the purpose. The unprecedented popularity of BELL, No. 1,—*four hundred thousand* having been issued and sold in the first twenty-four months of its publication,—and the urgent solicitation of Superintendents and Pastors of churches, have been the inducement for the preparation of the present volume. Nearly *thirty-five thousand* copies of this volume have been ordered in advance of publication; and the first edition will contain not less than *fifty thousand copies*. The editor has been cheered, likewise, with the information of numerous conversions of souls by means of the hymns and music of the former volume; it is his prayer and hope that the issue of this volume, and the circulation of its many evangelical sentiments and persuasions will be not less honored by the Saviour of men, in the great work of preparing multitudes to sing the New Song in glory.

There was a time when even David could not find an *old* song to express his emotion, and he exclaimed, "Praise ye the Lord; sing unto the Lord a NEW SONG · I will sing, yea, I will *sing* praises to God."

AND

SINGING OF THE GOSPEL BY ANGELS. CANTATA.

Luke ii. 8-13.

Music by A. Cull.

1ST VOICE. Alto Solo.

And there were in the } some country . . . } shepherds a - biding in the field, Keeping watch o - ver their flocks by

Piano or Organ.

2D VOICE. Soprano Solo.

night, And lo! the angel of the Lord came up - on them, { And the glory of the } Lord shone . . . } round a -

f Slow.

- bout them, And they were sore a - fraid. And the an - gel said un - to them,

"Fear not. Fear not!"

Terzetto. (Soprano and two Altos.)

2

Moderato.   p 1st time.   f 2d time.

3D VOICE.

Fear not! Fear not, for be-hold! I bring you good tidings of great joy which will be to all

Piano.

Allegretto.
4th VOICE.   Alto or Soprano.   (Joyfully.)

1st time.   2d time.

peo - - - ple, Oh!   peo - - ple!   For un - to you   is   born this day, in the

Rit.

cit - y   of   Da - vid,   &   Sa   viour, which is Christ the Lord, which is Christ the Lord.

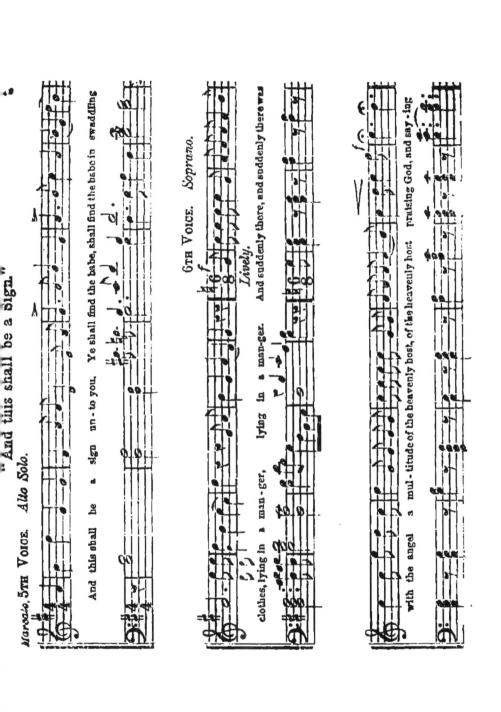

6

DON'T YOU HEAR THE ANGELS COMING?

Music by Rev. Robert Lowry.   Arr. by H. Waters.

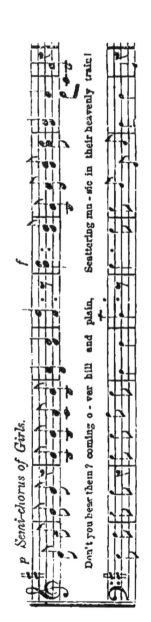

Duett.   *Soprano and Alto.*

1. Holy angels in their flight, Traverse over earth and sky, Acts of kindness their delight, Winged with mercy as they fly,

p Semi-chorus of Girls.

Don't you hear them? coming o - ver hill and plain,   Scattering mu - sic in their heavenly train!

Chorus.

Oh! don't you hear the angels coming, singing as they come? Oh! bear me angels, angels bear me home.

2

Tho' their forms we cannot see,
They attend and guard our way,
Till we join their company
In the fields of heavenly day.
Cho.—Don't you hear, &c

Had we but an angel's wing,
And an angel's heart of flame,
Oh, how sweetly would we ring
Thro' the world the Saviour's name.
Cho.—Don't you hear, &c.

3.

Yet methinks if I should die,
And become an angel, too,
I, perhaps, like them might fly,
And the Saviour's bidding do.
Cho.—Don't you hear, &c

JESUS.*

Solo.

Music by B. W. Williams.

Solo.

1. Who was in the manger laid? Je - sus. Who for money was betrayed? Je - sus.
2. Who can hear us when we call? Je - sus. Who the dearest friend of all? Je - sus.

Who up Cal - va - ry was led? Who for us his life-blood shed? Jesus Christ, creation's head.
Who a - lone can do us good, When we're tossed on Jordan's flood? Jesus Christ, our risen Lord.

3. Who can rob the grave of gloom?
   Jesus.
   Who can raise us from the tomb?
   Jesus.
   When before the Judge we wait,
   Who will open heaven's gate?
   Jesus Christ, our Advocate.

4. Who will give us sweetest rest?
   Jesus.
   Whom in heaven shall we love best?
   Jesus.
   At his feet our crowns we'll fling,
   While the rapturous song we sing,
   Jesus Christ, our Saviour King.

* From Songs for the Sabbath School and Vestry, by permission of H. Hoyt, Publisher.

BRIGHT, HAPPY NEW YEAR

Tune, "Prairie Flower." page 9.

1. On this New Year evening, when our hearts are
All around us cheerful, gay, and bright, [light
With our happy voices let us fill the air,
And a Father's love declare.
Merrily we sing, then, children, one and all,
Praise your bounteous Giver, great and small,
For the many mercies daily he bestows,
From the dawn till evening's close.

CHORUS.

Bright, happy New Year! joyful we sing.
Hearts full of gladness now we bring;
Take the e offerings, Jesus, full of love and cheer,
Smile upon the glad New Year.

2. Come, dear children, join our happy little band,
Pressing onward to the "better land,"
Where the angels welcome, with their harps of gold,
All the lambs of Jesus' fold.
In the land of sunshine sorrow is unknown,
All is calm and peaceful round the throne;
Come ye sad and weary to this place of rest.
Come and be forever blest.

CHORUS.

Bright, happy New Year! joyful we sing, &c.

NOT GREENLANDS ICY MOUNTAINS.

Tune, "Missionary Hymn," 7s & 6s, peculiar.

1. Not Greenland's icy mountains,
Nor India's coral strand;
No dark, or sunny fountains,
In any pagan land,
Calls louder to deliver
Their souls from error's chains,
Than here, by sea and river,
In all our streets and lanes

2. What though our Christian altars
Are raised in costly style,
If Christian courage falters,
Nor strives to save the vile:
In vain has God in kindness,
His blessings on us strown,
Where, in heathen blindness,
Men live, unblessed, unknown.

3. Was Priest or Levite lighted,
With wisdom from on high,
Who turned aside, and slighted
A fallen brother's cry?
Salvation! O Salvation!
To sinners here proclaim,
The poor of every nation
Must learn Messiah's name.

4. Then waft, ye winds, his story,
And you, ye waters, roll,
Till like a sea of glory,
It spreads from pole to pole,
Till o'er our ransomed nature,
The Lamb for sinners slain,
Redeemer, King, Creator,
In bliss returns to reign.

The above hymn was arranged for the use of Five Points Gospel Union Mission, 42 Baxter Street, New York, by W. S. W.

DOXOLOGY.

Praise God, from whom all blessings flow!
Praise him, all creatures here below!
Praise him above, ye heavenly host!
Praise Father, Son, and Holy Ghost!

ROUSE THEE, CHILD OF HEAVEN!

Words by Rev. Sidney Dyer.

Music by G. F. Root, by permission. Arr. by A. Cull.

Duet.

1. Rouse thee, child of heaven! why despairing thought? God to thee has giv - en, all unsought,
D. S. Bright, and fadeless glories in the world a - bove,......

CHORUS to each verse.

Pledge of his e - ter - nal love! Trust him for - ev - er! rest in his word; Grace he has giv - en,

prayer he has heard; Shout in notes of gladness, let thy spir - it soar, Praising h' - m for - ev - er - more!

Glowing on the hill side, blushing in the flowers,
Happy spirits greet us, cheering ours;
Cease from thy re - pining, rouse thee, child of heaven!
Share the blessin.. oul has given. Trust him, &c.

Rouse thee from thy sadness, rouse thee, drooping soul,
Anthem notes of gladness round thee roll;
Catch the song of rapture, join the seraph strain,
Healing all thy care and pain. Trust him, &c.

9

18

MUSIC OF ANGELS.

Words by Mrs. M. A. Kidder
Music arranged by A. Gull

Allegretto.

"DUET. 1st Voice.

1st Voice. I hear not a foot - - step, there is not a

2d Voice. There is not a foot - - step, but list to the

Repeat.

tone To cheer me in sadness when wen - ry and lone;

song, Sweet an - gels are sing - ing a glo - ri - fied throug;

1st Voice.

2d Voice.

Hark! the soft cho - rus un-ceas - ing - ly rolls, Glo - ry to Je - sus, Re-

Both. A tempo.

Rit.

deem - - er of souls, What can be dear - er in heav - en a - bore, Than

MUSIC OF ANGELS. Concluded.

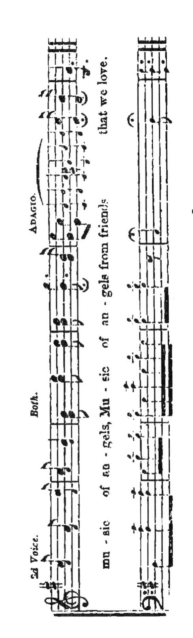

2.

In dreams as I listen, in tones sweet and clear,
The music of heaven strikes soft on my ear;
My rapturous spirit unites in the strain,
To worship, with angels, the Lamb that was slain!
Hark! the soft music, &c.

3.

O! grant me, dear Father, when death draweth near,
The "music of angels" may fall on my ear;
The foretaste of rapture my spirit shall know,
When meeting the friends I have loved here below.
Hark! the soft music, &c.

12

IS IT TRUE? 7s.

MALVROSA   Words by Horace Lidd, Esq.

Music by M. F. H. Smith.

1. Is it true that I must lie,   In the grave-yard by and by, And with oth-ers, gone be-fore,

Chorus Ritard.

Sleep till time shall be   no more? Is   it true—Oh! is   it true? Is   it true? Is   it true—Oh! Is   it true?

2 Is it true, as many say,
Life is but a passing day,
And that heaven is lost or won
Ere this fleeting day has flown?
  Is it true—Oh! is it true?

3 Is it true that on the cross.
Jesus bled and died for us,
And, while hanging on the tree.
Upward sent a prayer for me!
  Is it true—Oh! is it true?

4 Is it true that all death's slain,
Will arise and live again,
And to final judgment go,
Some for bliss and some for woe
  Is it true—Oh! is it true?

AND WHO CAN TELL.

Tranquillo. Words by Rogers Ruff, Esq.

Music Arr. by M. T. H. Smith

The flowery field of youth th' trod, On which her eye de-light-ed led; The Saviour called, "For-

... sake your toys!" She would not lis-ten to his voice—And who can tell? And who can tell?

CHORUS.

2 The spring-time quickly passed away
   From off the hill side and the dell;
   And then, we saw her pressed with cares,
   Unmindful of her soul's affairs—
        And, who can tell?

3 When on her dying bed she lay,
   She dreamed she heard the funeral knell·
   "A little longer!" then she cried,
   "A year! a day!" and so she died—
        Ah!—who can tell?

4 Fain would we hope when o'er the grave
   Her spirit hovered, all was well,
   That, at the last, the Saviour smiled,
   And owned the sufferer as his child,
        But, who can tell?

5 Then, seek the Saviour in thy youth,
   Early thy sinful passions quell?
   Now for the better world prepare,
   For death may come ere you're aware—
        And, who can tell?

14

THE PLEASANT SABBATH SCHOOL.

Words by Mrs. M. A. Kidder. Arr. by A. Cull.

Allegretto.
Duet.

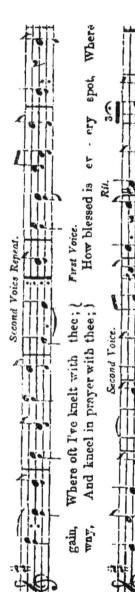

1st Voice. When light comes o'er the plain, And sunshine o'er the lea, Oh! meet me once a -
2d Voice. When first the sun's bright ray, Illumes the sparkling sea, I'll leave my homeward

Second Voice Repeat.

First Voice.

gain, Where oft I've knelt with thee; How blessed is ev - ery spot, Where
way, And kneel in prayer with thee;

Second Voice.

Rit.

we in youth have prayed, Where sweet and sacred thought, Each hour so blissful made.

The pleas - ant Sab - bath school, To us a ho - ly place, With -

At morning's rosy hour,
On each blest Sabbath day,
Oh! leave thy pleasant bower,
And come where Christians pray.

I'll sing the blessed songs,
The dear inspiring strains,
Whose sweetest song belongs
To Christ our Lord, who reigns.
How blest is every spot, &c.

16

YOUTHFUL DAYS.

Words and Music by HASTINGS.

CHANT-LET.

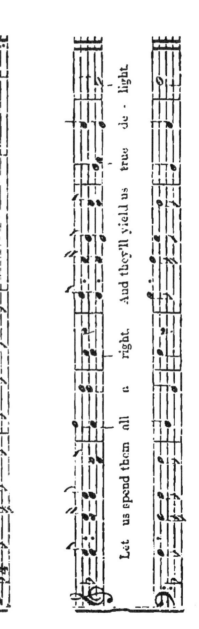

1. { Youthful days when bright and cheer - ful, Nev - er should be i - dly spent; }
   { Nor when gloomy, dark, and tear - ful, Should they lead to dis - con - tent; }

Let us spend them all a right, And they'll yield us true de - light

2 Youthful days will soon be over,
   Though they seem to linger long ;
   Time once past we ne'er recover,
   Whether we are old or young;
   Though we may its loss deplore,
   It has fled forevermore.

3 Youthful days are few and precious,
   Let us then our time improve ;
   And may God, forever gracious,
   Fill us with a Saviour's love ;
   That will keep us day by day
   Safe along the heavenly way.

COME TO JESUS.

Arranged, and partly composed by H. WATERS.

ALLEGRETTO.

1. Come to Je-sus, Come to Je-sus, Come to Je-sus, Come to Je-sus, Just now, Just now, Come to Je-sus, Just now!
2. He will save you, He will save you, He will save you, He will save you, Just now, Just now, He will save you, Just now!
3. I be-lieve it, I be-lieve it, I be-lieve it, I be-lieve it, Just now, Just now, I be-lieve it, Just now!
4. I am hap-py, I am hap-py, I am hap-py, I am hap-py, Just now, Just now, I am hap-py, Just now!
5. Hal-le-lu-jah, Hal-le-lu-jah, Hal-le-lu-jah, Hal-le-lu-jah, Just now, Just now, Hal-le-lu-jah, Just now!

17

ALLEGRETTO.   THE CHILDREN'S WELCOME.   Music by J. R. Osgood.

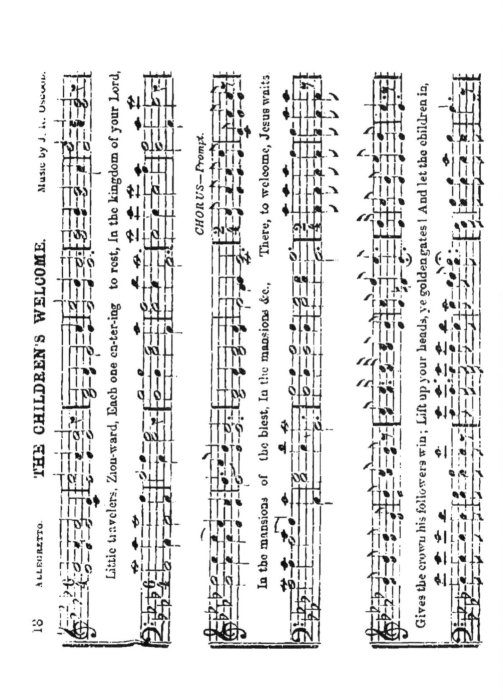

Little travelers, Zion-ward, Each one en-ter-ing to rest, In the kingdom of your Lord,

CHORUS—Prompt.

In the mansions of the blest, In the mansions &c.,   There, to welcome, Jesus waits

Gives the crown his followers win; Lift up your heads, ye golden gates! And let the children in,

Lift up your heads, Lift up your heads, Lift up, &c., ye golden gates, And let the children in.

2.
Who are they, whose little feet,
Pacing life's dark journey through,
Now have reached that heavenly seat,
They had ever kept in view.
　There, to welcome, Jesus waits, &c.

3.
"I from Greenland's frozen land,"
"I from India's sultry plain,"
"I from Afric's burning sand,"
"I from islands of the main,"
　There, to welcome, Jesus waits, &c.

4.
"All our earthly journey past,
Every tear and pain gone by,
Here together met at last,
At the portal of the sky!"
　There, to welcome, Jesus waits, &c.

5.
Each the welcome "Come" awaits,
Conqueror's over death and sin;
Lift up your heads, ye golden gates!
Let the little travelers in.
　There, to welcome, Jesus waits, &c.

THE PRIVILEGE.

WORDS AND MUSIC BY DR. HASTINGS

3. The lessons ye give us, seem hard to learn.
We often feel langund and dull;
And then are impatient and wish to turn
Away from the Sabbath school;
The lessons grow easy to all who try,
And moments fly swift when zeal runs high.

4. Oh' waken to industry then we say,
We'll faithfully, cheerfully try;
And courage and effort shall win the day,
And fill up the moments with joy;
Yet tenderly think of the name we love,
Acknowledge your sin, and grateful prove.

Duet.

NEVER FORGET THE SABBATH SCHOOL.

Teachers.
Never forget the Sabbath school, The lessons taught you here, The gentle words of kindness, The true and earnest care.

Remember, too, the teachers, Who oft for you will pray, That Jesus, by his gracious love, May keep you in the way.

CHORUS.

Never forget, Never forget, Never forget the Sabbath school, The lessons taught you here, The lessons &c.

Never forget the Sabbath school, &c.

Children. Can we forget the Sabbath school.
The place of light and love,
Place where we learn of wisdom's ways,
That leads to homes above?
Wherever we may wander,
Where through the week we roam,
We'll not forget the teachers
Of this, our Sabbath home.
Never forget, never forget,
Never forget the teachers
Of this, our Sabbath ho——

All. So, then, together let us sing.
In song of grateful praise,
To Him who reigneth in the skies
Our grateful tribute raise.
And pray that through another year
His blessing may attend:
And that we never may forget
The sinner's truest friend.
Never forget, never forget,
Never forget that Jesus is
The sinner's truest friend.

22

VIVACE.   A LIGHT IN THE WINDOW FOR THEE.   Music by A. Cull.

NOTE.—When a boy, but twelve years old, I worked hard to support my mother and two younger brothers, and usually carried my earnings home every evening. One night, it being very dark and muddy, and having three miles to travel, and a heavy bundle to carry, I did not reach home until late: my mother, feeble and weary, had retired, but she quickly aroused when she heard my voice, and soon met me at the door, with a warm kiss, and warmer tears, and a "God bless you, my dear boy." As she received my bundle, she exclaimed, "After this, my son, I'll set a light in the window for you," and true to her word, the bright light in the window appeared, and Oh! how it cheered my heart ever after for years. Health failing me, I left home, (after my brothers could help mother), and went to sea. When three years from home, and on the Pacific Ocean, my mother died; but just before she expired, she said to those around her, "O give Edward my dying blessing, for he has been a good boy. Tell him I have gone to Heaven, and I will set a light in the window for him."

1. There's a light in the window for thee, dear brother, There's a light in the window for thee;
2. There's a crown, and a palm, dear brother, When your la-bors have ceased to be;
3. O watch, and be faith-ful, and pray, dear brother, All your journey o'er life's troubled
4. Then on! per-se-ver-ing-ly on, dear brother, Till from conflict and suf-fer-ing

thee;   Your mother has moved to her mansion above, There's a light in the window for
be;   For Je-sus has gone to prepare you a home, With a light in the
sea,   Tho' afflictions assail you, and storms beat severe, There's a light in the
free.   Bright angels are beckoning you over the stream, There's a light in the

window for
window, &c.
window, &c.
window, &c.

A LIGHT IN THE WINDOW FOR THEE.—Concluded.

thee. A man-sion in heaven we see,

we see,

And a light in the window for thee.

Tune, STAR OF THE EVENING, *page* 114, *"S. S. Bell."*

1. Shepherds, keeping watch by night.
Saw around a glorious light;
Heard an angel then proclaim,
"Christ is born in Bethlehem,"
Christ is born in Bethlehem.

CHORUS.

Christ is born, Christ is born.
Christ is born—is born in Bethlehem.

2. Soon by many a heavenly tongue
"Glory be to God" was sung,
"Peace on earth, good will to men,
Christ is born in Bethlehem."
Christ is born, Christ is born, &c.

3. Joyful tidings to mankind!
Richest grace they now can find;
Children, too, this grace may claim,
Christ is born in Bethlehem.
Christ is born in Bethlehem, &c.

4. Oh! how great his grace and love,
Thus to leave his throne above;
Thus to be our guilt and shame,
And be born in Bethlehem.
Christ is born in Bethlehem, &c

Tune, STAR OF THE EVENING.

WORDS BY MRS. M. A. KIDDER.

1. Bethlehem star, sweet gem of light,
Sent to guide our souls aright.
Wanderers from the Lord afar;
Star of the Christian, Bethlehem star.
Star of the Christian, Bethlehem star.

CHORUS.

Bethlehem star, Bethlehem star.
Star of the Christian, Bethlehem, Bethlehem star.

2. Shepherds, wondering, saw thee rise.
Glorious in the eastern skies;
Herald of a Saviour's birth,
Jesus, Lord of heaven and earth.
Bethlehem star, &c.

3. Radiant star! thy beams divine.
Bright with heavenly lustres shine;
Sinners from their God afar,
Look to the Christians guiding star
Bethlehem star, &c.

4. When all earthly scenes shall fade;
And we near death's silent shade,
Jesus, loved star, Oh light our way,
To realms above of perfect day.
Bethlehem star, &c.

THE ANGELS' SONG.

CHORUS.

2 "Tis a song for children, too;
  To the Saviour 'tis their due:
Let its grateful notes ascend to Him again;
Join with angels in their song,
And the heavenly strain prolong,
"Glory be to God, good will and peace to men."
Cho.—Through the earth, &c

3 Soon around that throne may we
  With those happy angels be,
Striking harps to strains that nevermore shall cease;
Mingling love with loftiest praise,
Still the chorus there we'll raise,
"Glory be to God, to men good will and peace"
Cho.—Through the earth. &c.

SHALL WE MEET BEYOND THE RIVER?

Music by G. H. Baker, Arr. by A. Cull.

25

Allegretto.

1. Shall we meet be - yond the riv - er, Where the sur - ges cease to roll, Where in all the
2. Shall we meet in that blest har - bor, When our stormy voyage is o'er? Shall we meet and
3. Shall we meet in yon - der cit - y, Where the towers of crys - tal shine, Where the walls are

bright for - ev - er, Sor - row ne'er shall press the soul?
cast the an - chor, By the fair ce - les - tial shore?
all of jas - per, Built by workman - ship di - vine?

Chorus to each verse.

Shall we meet? Shall we meet?
Shall we meet? Shall we meet?
Shall we meet? Shall we meet?

Shall we meet beyond the riv - er, Where the sur - ges cease to roll?

Shall we meet? Shall we meet? Shall we meet beyond the riv - er?

Shall we, &c.
Shall, &c.
Shall, &c.

Where the music of the ransomed
Rolls its harmony around,
And creation swells the chorus,
With its sweet melodious sound?

Shall we meet with many a loved one,
That was torn from our embrace?
Shall we listen to their voices,
And behold them face to face?

Shall we meet with Christ our Saviour,
When he comes to claim his own?
Shall we know his blessed favor,
And sit down upon his throne?

JESUS, WE THY LAMBS WOULD BE.

C. A. MARVIN.

GLIDING MOVEMENT.—NOT TOO FAST.

1. Je - sus, we thy lambs would be, Humbly we would fol-low thee, Waiting for the joyful day, When all care will pass away, When the reaping time shall come, And angels shout the harvest home, When the reaping time shall come, And angels shout the harvest home.

2 Now the field with grain is white,
Now the day is dawning bright,—
Brighter far the sky will be,
When our Master we shall see,
When the reaping time, &c.

3 May we wait, and watch, and pray,
For the coming of that day,
When the wheat shall sifted be,
And the chaff be driven from thee:
When the reaping time, &c.

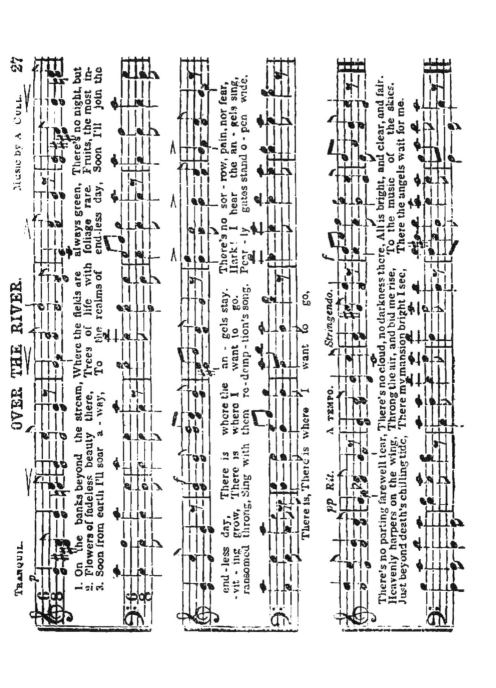

OVER THE RIVER.

TRANQUIL.

MUSIC BY A. CULL.

27

1. On the banks beyond the stream, Where the fields are always green, There's no night, but
2. Flowers of fadeless beauty there, Trees of life with foliage rare, Fruits, the most in-
3. Soon from earth I'll soar a - way, To the realms of end-less day, Soon I'll join the

end-less day, There is where the an - gels stay. There's no sor - row, pain, nor fear,
- vit - ing grow, There is where I want to go. Hark! I hear the an - gels sing,
ransomed throng, Sing with them re-demp-tion's song. Pear - ly gates stand o - pen wide.

There is, There is where I want to go.

PP Rit.   A TEMPO.   Stringendo.   f

There's no parting farewell tear, There's no cloud, no darkness there, All is bright, and clear, and fair.
Heavenly harpers on the wing, Throng the air, and bid me rise, To the music of the skies.
Just beyond death's chilling tide, There my mansion bright I see, There the angels wait for me.

THEY GATHERED ROUND THE CROSS.

CHORUS. Music by C. A. G.

4 VOICES.

* SINGLE VOICE.

1. They gathered | round the | cross.   Who | gathered | round?
2. They gathered | round the | cross   Who | gathered | round?

The lepers cleansed, the
The poor that heard his

blind restored to sight,   Captives of Sa - tan with their chains unbound, The dead called from the
ward, the hungry fed,   The broken-hearted healed of ev-ery wound; They to whose arms he

grave to life and light, The dead called from the grave to life and light,
restored the dead, They to whose arms he had restored the dead

They gathered | round the | cross.   Who | gathered | round?
    The lost reclaimed, sinners their sins forgiven,
    Who publicans whose eyes, that sought the ground,
    His hand had pointed to a smiling heaven.

They gathered | round the | cross.   Who | gathered | round?
    Women whose joy had been to soothe his woes,
    His mother—anguish, triumph, in each wound—
    Her Son, her Saviour, suffered for his foes.

They gathered | round the | cross.   Who | gathered | round?
    False priests that laughed, soldiers who mocked his pain,
    Proud Pharisees " whose garments swep the ground ",
    And thus upon the cross the Lord was slain.

Soft* { They gathered | round the | cross: He | closed his | eyes:
        The day grew dark when death its work had done:
Full { Yet day so bright ne'er dawned on mortal eyes,
        For our salvation by the cross was won.

* Sing first lines of last verse of Hymn all to first half of Chant, omitting the second half.

Tune, "Sweet Home."

WORDS BY REV. C. W. DENISON.

1. Oh! turn not the Sailor away from your door,
'Though poor, sick, and ragged he wander the shore,
He's a man, he's a brother, and oft you will find
Beneath a tarr'd Jacket a generous mind.
No, no, turn not away,
Oh, turn not the Sailor away from your door.

2. Oh, turn not the Sailor away from your door,
Though you see him but once, and may see him no
more;
For a poor suffering stranger was Jesus, our Lord,
And the cup of cold water shall have its reward.
No, no, turn not away, &c.

3. Oh, turn not the Sailor away from your door.
Though many a wild one has asked you before;
Perchance he has battled the ocean for you,
Where the wild billows raged, and the fierce tempest blew.
No, no, turn not away, &c.

4. Oh, turn not the Sailor away from your door,
Some strange, distant land you may yet wander o'er
To seek, lone and hungry, as weary you roam,
The grateful repose of a true Sailor's home.
No, no, turn not away, &c.

5. Oh, turn not the Sailor away from your door,
He may love the same God you have worshipp'd of
yore,
And when in the presence of angels you rest,
He may reign at your side in the land of the blest.
No, no, turn not away, &c.

Tune, "Antioch."

1. The Sailor's home is on the wave,
And there his grave will be;
Oh, Christian, stretch your hand, and save
This pilgrim of the sea.

2. O haste ye, for his life is brief;
Those "wild waves," booming free,
May sink to everlasting death
The pilgrim of the sea.

3. His heart is generous, kind, and brave—
Landsman, he toils for thee;
For thee he finds an early grave,
Lone pilgrim of the sea.

4. Jesus has pledged a bright reward
To those who'd faithful be,
And blest are they who turn to God
One pilgrim of the sea.

DO GOOD FOR THE SAILOR.

WORDS BY REV. C. W. DENISON.

1. Do good! do good! there's ever a way—
A way where there's ever a will;
Don't wait 'till to-morrow, but do it to-day,
And to-day, when to-morrow comes, still;
Do good to the Sailor, doomed often to roll
On billows of sorrow and need:
Embrace him with love, and his generous soul
Shall fill well repay you the deed.

CHORUS.

Then do good! do good! there's ever a way—
A way where there's ever a will, a will;
Don't wait 'till to-morrow, but do it to day,
And to-day, when to-morrow comes, still.

2. On shore, or at sea, when the Sailor you meet—
Oh! pass him not by in disdain;
Be tender and kind, as his spirit you greet—
God bless the brave son of the Main!
Then pity the Sailor—remember his fate
Is often so sad and forlorn;
Direct him to enter at mercy's straight gate,
Where Christ all his sorrows has borne.
Then do good! &c.

For tune to the above words, see "S. S. Bell," pp. 12 & 13.

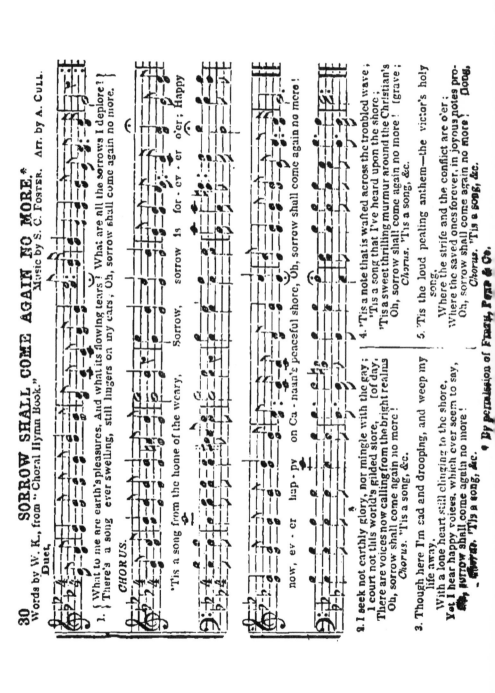

THANKS TO OUR FATHER IN HEAVEN.

Arr. by A. Cull.

HOSANNA TO THE LAMB OF GOD.

From "S. S. Minstrel."

Duet.

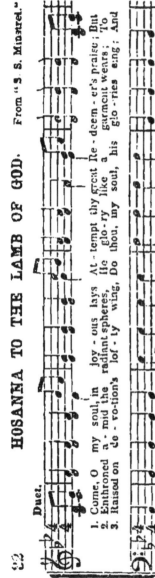

1. Come, O my soul, in joy - ous lays At - tempt thy great Re - deem - er's praise; But
2. Enthroned a - mid the radiant spheres, He glo - ry like a garment wears; To
3. Raised on de - vo - tion's lof - ly wing, Do thou, my soul, his glo - ries sing: And

CHORUS.

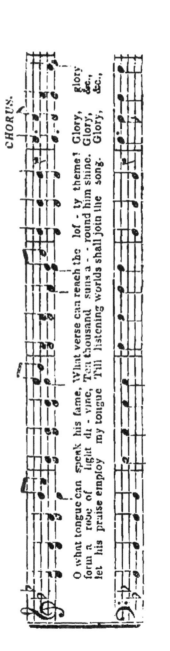

O what tongue can speak his fame, What verse can reach the lof - ty theme? Glory, glory,
form a robe of light di - vine, Ten thousand suns a - - round him shine. Glory, &c.,
let his praise employ my tongue Till listening worlds shall join the song. Glory, &c.,

let us sing, While heaven and earth with glory ring, Ho - san - na! Ho - - - san - na!

HOSANNA TO THE LAMB OF GOD.—CONCLUDED.

Allegretto.

Ho - san - na to the Lamb of God. Glo - ry, glo - ry, let us sing, While heaven and earth with

glo - ry ring, Ho - san - na! Ho - - - san - na! Ho - san - na to the Lamb of God.

---

1. JESUS shall reign where'er the sun
Does his successive journeys run;
His kingdom stretch from shore
Till moons shall wax and wane no more.
Glory, glory, &c.

2. People and realms of every tongue
Dwell on his love with sweetest song;
And youthful voices shall proclaim
Their early blessings on his name.
Glory, glory, &c.

3. Let every creature rise and bring
Peculiar honors to our KING;
Angels ascend with songs again,
And earth repeat the loud Amen.
Glory, glory, &c.

1. ALMIGHTY Ruler of the skies,
Through all the earth thy name is spread;
And thine eternal glories rise
Above the heavens thy hands have made.
Glory, glory, &c.

2. Amidst thy temple children throng
To see their great Redeemer's face:
The Son of David is their song,
And loud hosannas fill the place.
Glory, glory, &c.

1. AWAKE, my tongue, thy tribute bring
To him who gave thee power to sing
Praise him who has all power above,
The source of wisdom and of love.
Glory, glory, &c.

2. Through each bright world above, behold
Ten thousand, thousand charms unfold;
Earth, air, and mighty seas combine
To speak his wisdom all divine.
Glory, glory, &c.

3. But in redemption, O what grace!
Its wonders, O what thought can trace!
Here wisdom shines forever bright;
Praise him, my soul, with sweet delight.
Glory, glory, &c.

34

CHILDOOD'S HAPPY HOURS.

Duet.   Words by J. S. Adams.

Music by Cheely.   Arr. by A. Cull.

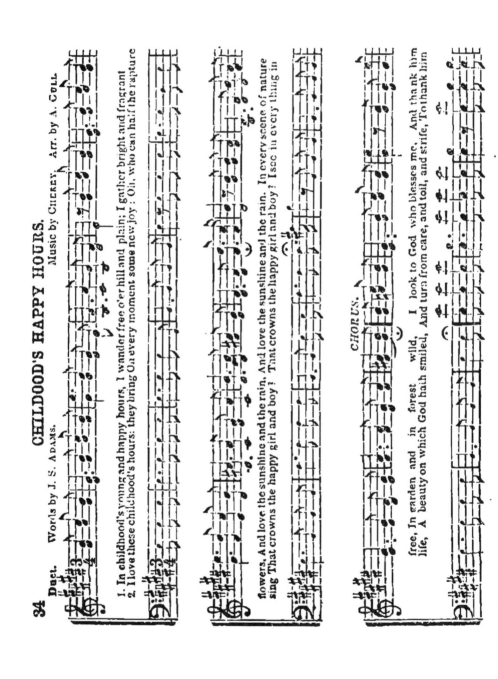

1. In childhood's young and happy hours, I wander free o'er hill and plain; I gather bright and fragrant
2. I love these childhood's hours: they bring On every moment some new joy: Oh, who can half the rapture

flowers, And love the sunshine and the rain. And love the sunshine and the rain. In every scene of nature
sing That crowns the happy girl and boy? That crowns the happy girl and boy? I see in every thing in

CHORUS.

free, In garden and in forest wild,   I look to God who blesses me,   And thank him
life, A beauty on which God hath smiled, And turn from care, and toil, and strife, To thank him

CHILDHOOD'S HAPPY HOURS.—CONCLUDED.

Rall.   Ad lib.

that I am a child, I look to God, who blesses me, And thank him that I am, I am a child
that I am a child, And turn from care, and toil, and strife, To thank him that I am, I am a child

This beautiful tune may be sung to any long metre hymn.

THE SUNDAY SCHOOL.

1. THE Sunday school, how dear to me!
   Within thy walls I love to be;
   Where, on the Sabbath day, we meet
   In our accustomed class and seat.

2. 'Tis there that I am taught to read
   God's holy word, and feel the need
   Of quickening grace and pardoning love,
   To fit me for yon heaven above.

3. 'Tis there that I am taught to pray,
   And love God's holy Sabbath day;
   To sing his praise and learn his will,
   And all my duties to fulfil.

4. Oh, let my songs and praises rise,
   Like grateful incense to the skies,
   For that rich grace, so free, so full,
   That brought me to the Sabbath school.

HOW LITTLE THINGS INCREASE.

1. A GRAIN of corn an infant's hand
   May plant upon an inch of land,
   Whence twenty stalks might spring and yield
   Enough to stock a little field.

2. The harvest of that field might then
   Be multiplied to ten times ten,
   Which sown twice more could furnish bread
   Wherewith an army might be fed.

3. A penny is a little thing,
   Which e'en a poor man's child may bring
   Into the treasury of Heaven,
   And make it worth as much as seven.

4. As seven! yea worth its weight in gold,
   And *that* increased an hundred fold,
   For lo! a penny tract, if well
   Applied, may save a soul from hell.

5. That soul can scarce be saved alone,
   It must, it will its bliss make known:
   Come, it will cry, and you shall see,
   What great things God hath done for me.

6. Hundreds that joyful sound shall hear,
   Hear with the heart as well as ear;
   And these to thousand more proclaim
   Salvation in the only name.

SISTER SPIRIT, STAY NOT HERE.

Words and Music by C. Hatch Smith, A. M.

ANDANTINO.

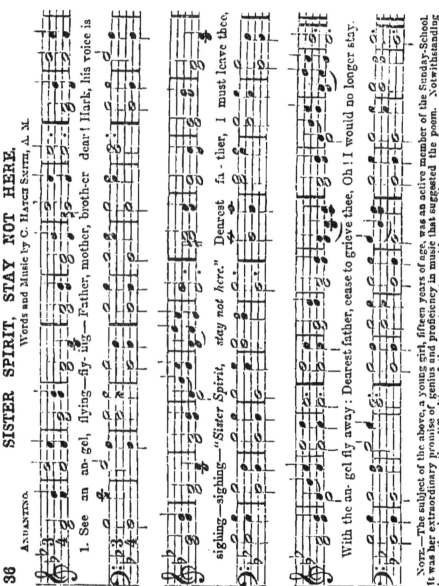

1. See an an-gel, flying—fly-ing— Father, mother, broth-er dear! Hark, his voice is sighing—sighing—"Sister Spirit, *stay not here.*" Dearest fa - ther, I must leave thee, With the an- gel fly away : Dearest father, cease to grieve thee, Oh ! I would no longer stay.

NOTE.—The subject of the above, a young girl, fifteen years of age, was an active member of the Sunday-School. It was her extraordinary promise of genius and proficiency in music that suggested the poem. Notwithstanding her youth, she overcame the difficulties of the great masters with ease. She was to have united with the protestant church the Sunday subsequent to her decease.

2. Music—hear it! ringing—ringing—
Earth is dark—I cannot see—
Seraph voices singing—singing—
"Sister Spirit, 'tis for thee."
I can hear them, mother, listen!
They are smiling now on you;
And, how bright their faces glisten!
Oh! I know their love is true.

3. Vision? no! we're going—going—
Now the angel speaks to me;
"For thy trust while sowing—sowing—
Sister Spirit, thou art free."
Oh! a crown within the portal,
Held by hands so pure and white:
Brother dear, its gems immortal,
Shine with rays of matchless light.

4. Weep no more, dear mother—mother—
Angels soon will seek thine ear;
And so soft, oh! father, brother,
Whisper, Spirit, stay not here.
Now, farewell, I go—I leave thee,
With the angel fly away:
Dearest loved ones, cease to grieve thee,
For I can no longer stay.

I LOVE THE SABBATH SCHOOL.

ORIGINAL HYMN.   Words by Mrs. S. Allaire.

1. I love the Sabbath School—Heaven of rest;
I love the Sabbath School—Sacred and blest.
Here, when the morning chime,
Peals forth its merry rhyme,
Young hearts are beating time,
Kind hands are press'd.

CHORUS.

I love the Sabbath School—
Sabbath School, Sabbath School,
I love the Sabbath School,
Dear Sabbath School.

2. We are a happy band—Onward we move—
Seeking that better land—Where all is love.
Youth with its rosy hue,
Sweet dimpled childhood, too,
Drinking the holy dew,
Pure from above.
I love the Sabbath School, &c.

3. Oft in that favored spot Sweet place of prayer,
Earth and its cares forgot—Jesus is there.
He who, though Lord of all,
Marks but a sparrow's fall;
He listens to our call—
Yes, God is there.
I love the Sabbath School, &c.

4. Come to the Sabbath School, God calls to-day,
Drink from this little pool—Make no delay.
This is the humble place
Christ loves to own and bless:
Here seek your Sabbath rest—
Haste, haste away.
I love the Sabbath School, &c.

Tune, KIND WORDS, IN S. S. BELL, Page 24.

38

HEAVENLY FATHER GRANT THY BLESSING.

Devoutly. CHORUS.

Music and Words by L. Wilder. Arr. by H. Wattes.

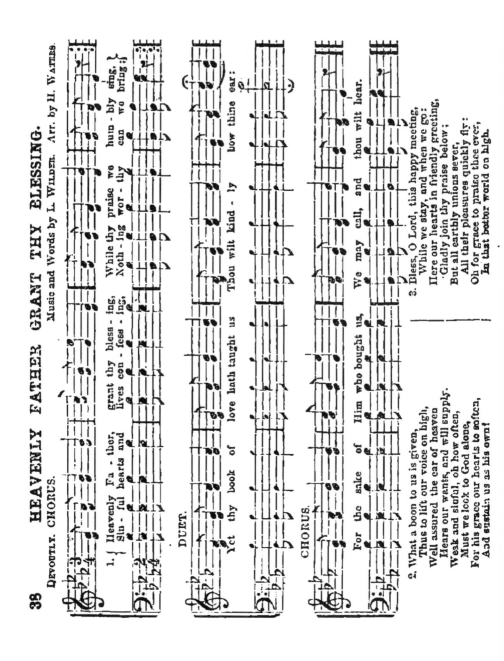

1. Heavenly Fa - ther, grant thy bless - ing, While thy praise we hum - bly sing, Sin - ful hearts and lives con - fess - ing, Noth - ing wor - thy can we bring;

DUET. Yet thy book of love hath taught us Thou wilt kind - ly low thine ear:

CHORUS. For the sake of Him who bought us, We may call, and thou wilt hear.

2. What a boon to us is given,
Thus to lift our voice on high,
Well assured the ear of heaven
Hears our wants, and will supply.
Weak and sinful, oh how often,
Must we look to God alone,
For his grace our hearts to soften,
And sustain us as his own!

3. Bless, O Lord, this happy meeting,
While we stay, and when we go:
Here our hearts in friendly greeting,
Gladly join thy praise below;
But all earthly unions sever,
All their pleasures quickly fly:
Oh for grace to praise thee ever,
In that better world on high.

JESUS, I MY CROSS HAVE TAKEN.

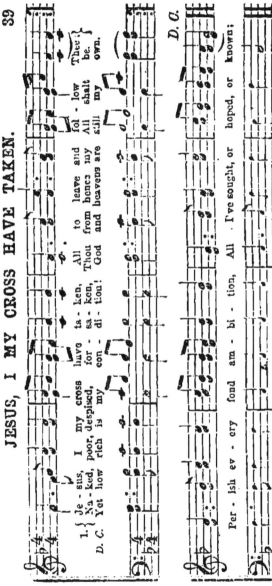

1. { Je - sus, I my cross have ta - ken,
D. C. Na - ked, poor, despised, for - sa - ken,
Yet how rich is my con - di - tion!

All to leave and fol - low Thee;
Thou from hence my All shalt be.
God and heavens are still my own.

D. C.

Per - ish ev - 'ry fond am - bi - tion, All I've sought, or hoped, or known;

2. Let the world despise and leave me,
   They have left my Saviour, too:
   Human hearts and looks deceive me,
   Thou are not, like them untrue:
   And whilst Thou shalt smile upon me,
   God of wisdom, love, and might,
   Foes may hate, and friends may scorn me;
   Show Thy face, and all is bright.

3. Man may trouble and distress me,
   'T will but drive me to Thy breast:
   Life with trials hard may press me,
   Heaven will bring no sweeter rest.
   Oh! 't is not in grief to harm me,
   While Thy love is left to me;
   Oh! 'twere not in joy to charm me,
   Were that joy unmixed with Thee.

4. Soul, then know thy full salvation,
   Rise o'er sin, and fear, and care;
   Joy to find in every station
   Something still to do or bear.
   Think what Spirit dwells within thee;
   Think what Father's smiles are thine;
   Think that Jesus died to win thee;
   Child of heaven, can'st thou repine?

5. Haste thee on from grace to glory,
   Armed by faith, and winged by prayer;
   Heaven's eternal day's before thee,
   God's own hand shall guide thee there.
   Soon shall close thy earthly mission,
   Soon shall pass thy pilgrim days;
   Hope shall change to glad fruition,
   Faith to sight, and prayer to praise.

40

"I'LL AWAKE AT DAWN."

From "S. S. Minstrel."

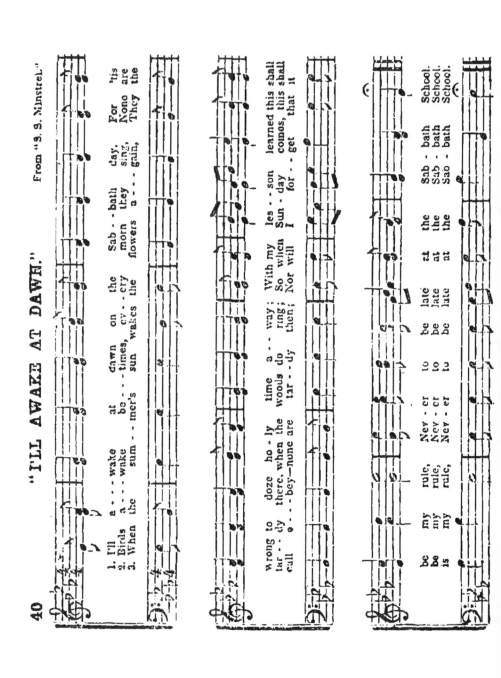

1. I'll a - - wake at dawn on the Sab - - bath day, For 'tis
2. Birds a - - wake be - - times, ev - - ery morn they sing, No no
3. When the sum - - mer's sun wakes the flowers a - - gain, They are

wrong to doze ho - ly time a - - way; With my les - - son learned this shall
tar - - dy there, when the woods do ring; So when Sun - day comes, this shall
call o - - bey—none are tar - - dy then; Nor will I for - - get that it

be my rule, Nev - er to be late at the Sab - bath School.
be my rule, Nev - er to be late at the Sab - bath School.
is my rule, Nev - er to be late at the Sab - bath School.

HOW PRECIOUS THE DYING OF SAINTS,

Words by Rev. SYDNEY DYER.

Music by J. R. OSGOOD.

1. How precious the dying of saints to the Lord, Who waits to receive them on high: And
2. To pilgrims, long wearied and sorely oppressed, Death comes as a precious boon given: And

they, with sweet rapture, attend thy glad word, And pant for their home in the sky, And they, &c., And
sweet are the accents which call to the rest, Prepared for the weary in Heaven! And sweet are, &c., Pre-

pant for their home in the sky, And they, with sweet rapture, attend the glad word. And pant. &c.
-pared for the weary in Heaven! And sweet are the accents which call to the rest, Prepared, &c.

3. The old and the young he enfolds in his arms,
   Unheeding the pleadings of love;
   But lo! to the righteous he opens those charms,
   Immortal and fadeless above!

4. Then, let us, rejoicing in Faith, ever sing,
   "I would not live always below,"
   Since Death plumes for Heaven with angels' bright [wing,
   I'm long, yea, panting, to go!

SPEAK GENTLY.

42

Music Arr. by A. Cull.

1. { Speak gen-tly it is better far, To rule by love than fear;
     { Speak gen-tly let no harsh words mar, The good we might do here.
D.C. Teach it in accents soft and mild From e-vil to re-frain. *Fine.*

Speak gen-tly to the lit-tle child, Its love be sure to gain; *D.C. al Fine.*

2.

Speak gently to the young, for they
Will have enough to bear;
Pass through this life as best they may,
'Tis full of anxious care.
Speak gently to the aged one,
Grieve not the careworn heart:
The sands of life are nearly run.
Let such in peace depart.

3.

Speak gently, kindly, to the poor,
Let no harsh tones be heard;
They have enough they must endure
Without an unkind word.
Speak gently to the erring ones;
They may have toiled in vain;
Perchance unkindness made them so:
Oh, win them back again.

THE HAPPY CHRISTMAS MORN.

LIVELY. Words by ANNA R. BARKULOU.

Music by JONES. Arr. by H. WAITE.

1. The promised morning o'er us breaks, Majestic in array: The great Re-deem-er
2. When evening shadows thickly fall, Around life's closing day, When dearest friends un-

on Him takes, The garment of our clay. For Bethlehem's babe shall save from sin, Young
heeded call, Life's memories swept a-way: Our hearts shall thrill to *one* dear name, In

children yet unborn; And angels joy to usher in, The happy Christmas morn, The
gentle whispers borne, Sweet Saviour! Jesus! He who came Upon the Christmas morn, The

THE HAPPY CHRISTMAS MORN. CONTINUED.

44

Christmas morn, The happy Christmas morn, The Christmas morn, The happy Christmas morn.
Christmas morn, Upon the · · · · · · · · · · - Upon the · · · -

CHORUS. f

For Bethlehem's babe shall save from sin, Young children yet unborn; And angels joy to
Our hearts shall thrill to one dear name, In gentle whispers borne, Sweet Saviour! Jesus!

ush- er in, The hap-py Christmas morn, And an-gels joy to ush- er in, The
He who enme, Up- on the Christmas morn, Sweet Saviour! Jesus! He who came Up-

happy Christmas morn, The happy Christmas morn,
on the Christmas morn. Upon the Christmas morn.

The happy, &c.
Up - on, &c.

The happy Christmas morn.
Upon the Christmas morn.

THE BLESSED SABBATH MORN.

WORDS BY MRS. MARY A. KIDDER.

The Sabbath bell so gayly breaks,
In music soft and clear,
Majestic o'er the woods and lakes
Its welcome sounds we hear.
Fair children smile to usher in
The day by God upborne;
While thousands with the dawn begin
To bless the Sabbath morn,
  The Sabbath morn,
To bless the Sabbath morn,
  The Sabbath morn,
To bless the Sabbath morn,
Fair children smile to usher in
The day by God upborne,
And thousands with the dawn begin
To bless the Sabbath morn,
  To bless, &c.
  To bless, &c.

In many a lane and street obscure,
In many a wretched cot,
Among the sad and starving poor,
The Sabbath is forgot;
'Tis there the sweet and heavenly notes,
On angel pinions borne,
Around their priceless souls should float,
Each blessed Sabbath morn;
  The Sabbath morn,
Each blessed Sabbath morn.
  The Sabbath morn,
Each blessed Sabbath morn,
'Tis there the sweet and heavenly notes,
On angel pinions borne,
Around their priceless souls should float,
Each blessed Sabbath morn.
  Each, &c.
  Each, &c.

BE KIND TO THE LOVED ONES AT HOME.

Andante Espressivo.

Music by I. B. Woodbury, Arr. by H. Waters.

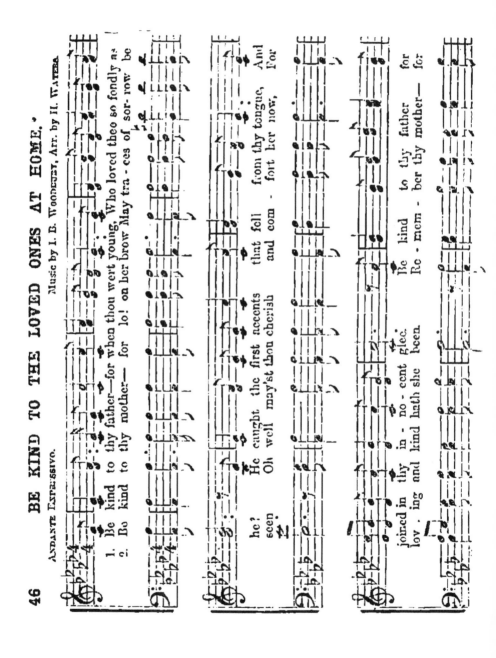

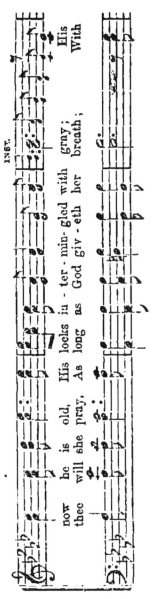

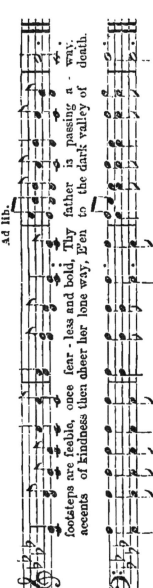

3. Be kind to thy brother—his heart will have dearth,
    If the smile of thy joy be withdrawn;
  The flowers of feeling will fade at their birth,
    If the dew of affection be gone.
  Be kind to thy brother—wherever you are,
  The love of a brother shall be
  An ornament purer and richer by far
  Than pearls from the depth of the sea.

4. Be kind to thy sister—not many may know
    The depth of true sisterly love;
  The wealth of the ocean lies fathoms below
    The surface that sparkles above.
  Be kind to thy father, once fearless and bold,
  Be kind to thy mother so near;
  Be kind to thy brother, nor shew thy heart cold,
  Be kind to thy sister so dear.

* By permission of O. Ditson and Co. Boston.

SELECTED HYMNS.

HEAVEN IS MY HOME.*

I'm but a stranger here,
 Heaven is my home.
Earth is a desert drear,
 Heaven is my home.
Dangers and sorrows stand,
Round me on every hand,
Heaven is my Father's land,
 Heaven is my home.

What though the tempests rage,
 Heaven is my home.
Short is my pilgrimage,
 Heaven is my home.
Time's cold and wintry blast,
Soon will be overpast,
I shall reach home at last,
 Heaven is my home.

What though the world allure,
 Heaven is my home.
Still is the promise sure,
 Heaven is my home.
Steadfast by faith I see,
Him who on Calvary,
Purchased this bliss for me.
 Heaven is my home.

Peace, Oh my troubled soul,
 Heaven is my home.
I soon shall reach the goal,
 Heaven is my home.
Swiftly the race I'll run,
Yield up my crown to none,
Forward, the prize is won,
 Heaven is my home.

* The tune to the above hymn may be found in Anniversary Book No. 3, p. 42. Price, 3 cents.

There at my Saviour's side,
 Heaven is my home.
I shall be glorified,
 Heaven is my home.
There are the good and blest,
Those I love most and best,
There, too, I soon shall rest,
 Heaven is my home

BE KIND TO THY PASTOR.

WORDS BY MRS. M. A. KIDDER.

Be kind to thy pastor—for many long years
 He's faithfully watched over thee;
He warns thee in mercy, entreats thee with tears,
 From sin and from error to flee.
Be kind to thy pastor—remember he bears
 A burden for me and for you;
Oh! make his work easy, and lighten his cares,
 By being both humble and true.

Be kind to thy teacher—for well dost thou know
 How kindly he labors for thee;
He minds not the tempest—he heeds not the snow,
 So tireless and earnest is he.
Be kind to thy teacher—that when thou dost stand
 By death's a silent river, alone,
The faith he hath taught thee may point to the land
 Where sorrow and pain is unknown.

Be kind to thy schoolmates, in good or in ill,
 Whatever the tempter may say;
Like you, they now stand at the foot of the hill,
 Young pilgrims in life's thorny way.
Be kind to thy schoolmates—be gentle and mild,
 The gift of sweet charity seek;
Remember that Jesus, who once was a child,
 Though tempted, was lowly and meek.

[Tune, "Be kind to the loved ones at home," p. 46.]

O GIVE THANKS UNTO THE LORD. Chant.

SOLO, OR SEMICHORUS. SUPERINTENDANT OR TEACHER. CHORUS BY THE SCHOOL AND CONGREGATION.

O give thanks unto the Lord, for he is good; For his mer-cy en - dur-eth for ev- er.

SOLO, OR SEMICHORUS.

CHORUS.

O give thanks unto the God of gods, For his mer-cy en-dur-eth for ev- er

A - men.

PSALM 136.

1. O give thanks unto the Lord, for he is good;   CHO. For his mercy endureth for ever.
2. O give thanks unto the God of gods;   CHO. For his mercy endureth for ever.
3. O give thanks unto the Lord of lords;   CHO. For his mercy endureth for ever.
4. To him who alone doth great wonders;   CHO. For his mercy endureth for ever.
5. To him that by wisdom made the heavens;   CHO. For his mercy endureth for ever.
6. To him that stretcheth out the earth above the waters; CHO. For his mercy endureth for ever.
7. To him that made great lights;   CHO. For his mercy endureth for ever.
8. The sun to rule by day; the moon and stars to rule by night; For his mercy endureth for ever.
9. Who remembered us in our low estate;   CHO. For his mercy endureth for ever.
10. And hath redeemed us from our enemies;   CHO. For his mercy endureth for ever.
11. Who giveth food to all flesh;   CHO. For his mercy endureth for ever.
12. O give thanks unto the God of heaven;   CHO. For his mercy endureth for ever. Amen.

By permission of W. B. Bradbury.

CALL THE CHILDREN EARLY, MOTHER.

Words by a Lady at the Rensselaer Street Mission, Albany.

Music by HENRY TUCKER.

1. Call the children ear - ly, mother, While the birds do sing, While the dew is on the flow - ers Which by the hill - side spring,

DUET. Oft repeat the waking word,

CHORUS. Till they rise to praise the Lord, Oft repeat the waking word, Till they rise to praise the Lord

2. Call the children early, father,
While the dew is on,
Great the work that must be done
Before the morning's gone:
Call them round the altar bright,
On which burns devotion's light,
Call them near the altar fair,

3. Call the children early, teacher,
From the paths of vice;
Every Sabbath day set forth,
The pearl of richest price:
Call them early to the Lord,
Thou shalt reap a rich reward,
Call them early, for

4. Call the children early, shepherd,
Give the lambs thy care;
See that they are folded safe
Within the house of prayer.
Call them at the dawn of day
Lead them in the narrow way,
Call them at the dawn, for

WHEN ON EARTH OUR DEAR REDEEMER.

Words and Music by J. R. Osgood.

SPRIGHTLY.

1. When on earth our dear Redeem-er, Made his home with sinful man;
2. Earn-est sought thy Jesus' presence, Earnest urged their suit of love:
3. "Suf-fer ye the lit-tle children, Let them ear-ly seek my grace,
4. Dearest Saviour, I would love thee, Thou thy love bestow on me;

Though his grace was oft re -
Plead- ing, Saviour bless our
Know ye not their an - gels
Make me clean from all trans-

None e'er sought that grace in vain;
Let them thy sweet mercies prove;
Gaze up - on my Father's face;
Meet to dwell in heaven with thee;

Some there were who sought his blessing, On their
Stern dis - ci - ples, round him gathered, Bade them
In His arms He did en - fold them, Gen - tly
Then in songs of ho - ly rap - ture Will I

. . ject - ed,
dear ones,
ev - er
gres sion,

children dear to rest,
from his presence flee;
pressing to His breast,
chant in glorious rays,

Knowing well, this boon possess- ing, They were rich-ly,
Je - sus turning, straight rebuked them, Saying "let them
And with words of heavenly kindness, Lulled their rising
While in our triumphant cho - rus, Saints and angels

tru - ly blest.
come to me."
fears to rest.
swell thy praise.

I'M WITH THEE STILL.

"Are they not all ministering spirits, sent forth to minister to those who shall be heirs of salvation?"

ANDANTE. Words by Mrs. A. M. Elmore.

Music by A. Gell.

1. Mother! sweet mother! though ma-ny a day Has pass'd like the swift winged clouds a-way, Since thou, with grief that was al-most wild, Didst give to the an-gel of death thy child : Nev-ermore let a tear thine eye-lid fill : For,

* Written on the death of Miss Lizzie Waters.

I'M WITH THEE STILL. (Concluded.)

mother! sweet mother! I'm with thee still! For, mother! sweet mother! I'm with thee still!

2.

Thou canst not see me, thy child so dear,
Thou canst not hear me, yet I am near,
I watch thee, mother, as thou didst me,
In the days of my youth, and my infancy.
Love's holiest vigil I come to fill,
Mother! dear mother! I'm with thee still

3.

When the east is red with the coming morn,
And the stars grow pale in the crimson dawn,
And the busy cares of a new-born day
Are chasing the shadows of sleep away,
Thy cup from the river of life I fill,
Mother! sweet mother! I'm with thee still

4.

When the sun goes down to his couch of gold,
And the shadowy wings of night unfold,
And the stars light up the beautiful road
That shows the path to the saint's abode,
I come with the angels who do his will—
Mother! dear mother! I'm with thee still

5.

I see thee kneel in the place of prayer,
And I fold my pinions in silence there,
As the earnest of faith to thee is given,
The hope that heralds the bliss of heaven,
And the holiest peace which the soul can fill—
Mother! sweet mother! I'm with thee still

6.

When the hour shall come, and thy strength shall fail,
And thy feet are turned to the narrow vale;
And the waters of death, so dark and cold,
Shall o'er *thee* roll as o'er *me* they rolled,
I will touch thy hand, in the waves so chill,
Mother! dear mother! I'm with thee still

7.

When the river is cross'd and the journey done,
The conflict is over, the vic'ry won.
And thy feet are firm on that glorious shore,
Where sorrow and parting are known no more,
Never more shall a tear thine eyelid fill.
There, there, sweet mother! I'm with thee still

THE TRUSTING PILOT, or TRUST IN HEAVEN.

J. R. OSGOOD.

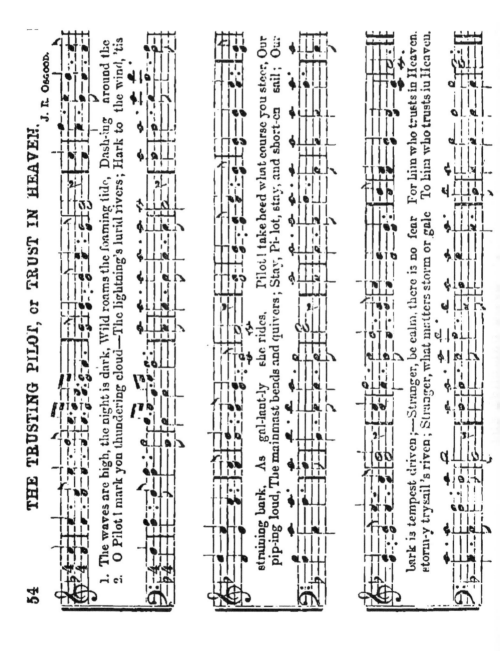

1. The waves are high, the night is dark, Wild roams the foaming tide, Dash-ing around the straining bark. As gal-lant-ly she rides. Pilot! take heed what course you steer, Our bark is tempest driven;—Stranger, be calm, there is no fear For him who trusts in Heaven.

2. O Pilot! mark yon thundering cloud—The lightning's lurid rivers; Hark to the wind, 'tis pip-ing loud, The mainmast bends and quivers; Stay, Pi-lot, stay, and short-en sail; Ou storm-y trysail's riven; Stranger, what matters storm or gale To him who trusts in Heaven.

3. Borne by the wind, the vessel flees
   Up to that thundering-cloud;
   Now tottering low, spray-winged seas
   Conceal the top-mast shroud;
   Pilot, the waves break o'er us fast,
   Vainly our bark has striven;
   Stranger, the Lord can rule the blast,
   Go, put thy trust in Heaven.

4. Good hope! good hope! one little star
   Gleams o'er the waste of waters;
   'T is like the light, reflected far,
   Of beauty's loveliest daughters.
   Stranger, good hope! He giveth thee.
   As He has always given—
   Then learn this truth, whate'er may be.
   To put thy trust in Heaven.

OUR PASTOR WE GREET.

Words by Hon. ROBERT H. PRUYN.

HENRY TUCKER.

1. Our Pas-tor we greet. As once more we meet To min-gle in prayer and in praise,
2. When the portals of gold For him shall unfold, The work of his Saviour well-done,
3. With ranks ev-er full, Let our Sabbath school The hope of the church ever be,

With him may we ev-er, Till death shall us sev-er, En-joy these glad festival days.
More than autumnal leaves May he bear home his sheaves, The crown of rejoicing then won,
As streams from the fountains, Far up in the mountains, Descending, fill river and sea.

CHRISTMAS BELLS ARE RINGING.

Words by M.   Music by Henry Tucker.

CHEERFULLY.

1st time Semi-Chorus, 2d time full Chorus.

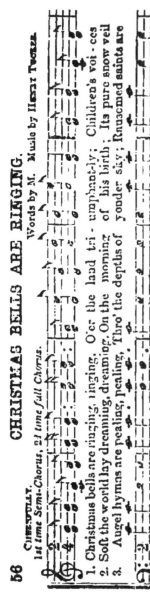

1. Christmas bells are ringing, ringing, O'er the land tri - umphant-ly; Children's voi - ces
2. Soft the world lay dreaming, dreaming, On the morning of his birth; Its pure snow veil
3. Angel hymns are pealing, pealing, Thro' the depths of yonder sky; Ransomed saints are

CHO. Christmas bells are ringing, ringing, O'er the land tri-umph-ant-ly; Children's voi - ces

Fine. DUET.

singing, singing, Sound a joyous ju - bi - lee.   'Tis the day the wondrous sign,
gleaming, gleaming, When the Christ-child came on earth. He's the priceless pearl we hail,
kneeling, kneeling, At the throne on high With grateful voi - ces come we now,

singing, singing, Sound a joyous ju - bi - lee.

Rit.

D. C.

Broke the wise men's calm repose; Newly robed in rays divine, The Star of Bethlehem arose.
Sent us from a Father's hand; A fount of life that shall not fail, A rock in a weary land.
Come, both heart and hand to lift; Lord of Life, to thee we bow, And thank thee for thy gift.

SABBATH BELLS ARE RINGING, RINGING.

1. Sabbath bells are ringing, ringing,
   Like soft voices, in the air,
   Of the angels, winging, winging,
   To the sacred house of prayer.
   'Tis the day of holy rest,
   When the world, with all its care,
   Shall not rule the anxious breast;
   God reigns triumphant there.
   Chorus—Sabbath bells, &c.

2. Children's voices, pealing, pealing,
   Are the echoes of their souls;
   When they worship, kneeling, kneeling,
   In their pleasant Sabbath schools.
   Lisps the blessed Saviour's name;
   There the teacher, bowed in dust,
   The cross his only claim.—*Chorus*.

3. Light from heaven beaming, beaming,
   Breaks in glory on the soul;
   Hope in beauty, gleaming, gleaming,
   Cheers the children's Sunday school.
   Light and hope, and faith and love,
   Peace and joy are their reward;
   Heavenly blessings from above,
   For children of the Lord.—*Chorus*.

G. W. BUNGAY.

SPRING BUDS SWEET ARE BLOOMING.

1. Spring-buds sweet are blooming, blooming,
   Fragrant spice-breath of the flowers,
   Spilled on cool winds, booming, booming,
   Drumming up the summer showers,
   Now foretell a plenteous year;
   May it bring God's loved ones near
   His throne to worship him.
   Chorus—Spring-buds sweet, &c.

2. Storm-winds loud are calling, calling,
   On the sobbing clouds to come;
   Autumn leaves are falling, falling,
   And the partridge taps her drum,

Soon the autumn of our days
Tinges life with soberness;
May it mellow in His rays,
The Sun of Righteousness.—*Chorus*.

3. Winter's cold is stinging, stinging,
   All the life it touches there;
   While the winds are flinging, flinging,
   Snow-flakes on the drifted hair.
   But there is a land above,
   Where will reign perpetual spring,
   Light of God's unchanging love,
   Beneath his sheltering wing.—*Chorus*.

G. W. BUNGAY.

WILD BIRDS NOW ARE SINGING, SINGING.

A SONG FOR PIC-NICS.

1. Wild birds now are singing, singing,
   In the woodlands, green and fair;
   Wood-notes now are ringing, ringing,
   From the tree-tops in the air.
   Sweet bird of the dusky wine,
   And the swelling breast of flame,
   When we hear thy sweet notes ring,
   Our praise is put to shame.
   Chorus—Wild birds now, &c.

2. Flowers here are clinging, clinging,
   To the rude rocks in the dell;
   They are kissed by springing, springing,
   Wavelets from the woodland well.
   As the sweet flowers breathe their balm
   On the crystal atmosphere,
   So the perfume of our psalm
   Shall sweeten offerings here.—*Chorus*.

3. Sunlight here is streaming, streaming,
   From the fountains in the sun,
   Blending here its beaming, beaming,
   Light with shadows as they run.
   Braiding thus the light and shade,
   Underneath the quivering leaves;
   So our chequered life is made,
   Where sun and shadow weaves.—*Chorus*.

G. W. BUNGAY.

"WHO WOULD NOT LOVE THE SUNDAY SCHOOL?"

Andante Cantabile.

CHORUS. Words and Music by M. F. H. Smith.

1. Who would not love the Sunday school? The place where youthful hearts are taught.
2. Who would not love the Sunday school? 'Tis there the Saviour loves to meet

To learn and love God's ho-ly word, To guide their no-tions, minds, and thoughts.
All lit-tle chil-dren and their friends, Who come his word to learn and teach.

3.

Who would not love the Sunday school?
'Tis there we all should love to go,
'Tis there we learn our Saviour's will,
'Tis there we learn his face to know.

4.

Who would not love the Sunday school?
'Tis there we learn of that dear Friend,
Who came and died for such as we,
And who will guide us to the end.

GOD'S FAVORS ACKNOWLEDGED.

Words and Music by P. H. Raffen.

1. Lord, we thank thee for the blessings Thou hast strewn along our way; Blessings, without stint or num-ber, We receive from day to day, We receive from day to day.

2.

In the morning, when the sunlight
Breaks along the eastern sky,
We behold the first bright dawning
Of the power of God on high.

3.

Through the day his mercy hovers
O'er us, in each shining hour,—
And when coming shades surround us,
Still we feel his sheltering power.

4.

Unseen angels in the darkness
Of the night surround our beds,
And the blessings of the Father
Rest upon our youthful heads.

5.

For thy gifts, O Lord, we thank thee,
For thy blessings and thy love;
And with words of joy we'll praise thee
Here, and in thy courts above.

THE MOTE AND BEAM.

Words by S. H.

Music by Rev. Mr. M   Arr. by A. Cull

60

1. Truth re - flects up - on the sens - es, Gos - pel light re - veals to some,

If there still should be of - fen - ces, Woe to him by whom they come.

"Judge not that ye be not judg - ed," Was the coun - sel Je - sus gave;

THE MOTE AND BEAM. (CONCLUDED.)

With what mea-sure you have giv-en, Just the same you shall re-ceive.

2. Jesus said, be meek and lowly,
    For 't is high to be a Judge,
    If I would be pure and holy,
    I must love without a grudge:
    It requires a constant labor,
    All these precepts to obey;
    If I truly love my neighbor,
    I am in the narrow way.

3. Once I said unto my neighbor,
    In thine eye there is a Mote,
    If thou art a friend or brother,
    Hold and let me pull it out;
    But I could not see it fairly,
    For my sight was very dim,
    When I came to see more clearly,
    In mine eye, there was a Beam.

4. If I truly love my neighbor,
    And this Mote I would erase,
    Then my light must shine more clearly;
    For the eye 's a tender place,

Others I have oft reproved,
    For a little simple Mote!
    Now I wish the Beam removed,
    Oh, that tears would wash it out!

5. Charity and love are healing,
    These will give a clearer sight,
    When I searched for others' failings,
    I was not exactly right.
    Now I'll take no further trouble,
    Jesus' love is all my theme;
    Little Motes are but a bubble,
    When compared unto a Beam!

6. In sweet union let us travel,
    Pilgrims through this world of woe,
    All upon one Christian level,
    None but Jesus will we know.
    Farewell then to disputation,
    Firm, united let us be,
    In love's highest dispensation,
    Live with Christ eternally.

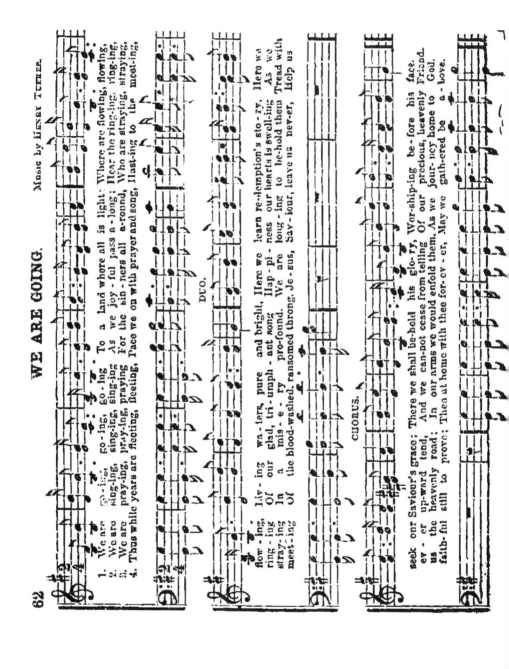

WE ARE GOING.

Music by HENRY TUCKER.

IN THE ROSY LIGHT.

Music by Henry Tucker. 83

Semi-Chorus.

1. In the ro - sy light of the morning bright Lift the voice of praise on high; From the lips of youth to the
2. Let his praise be spread for the Lamb who bled To deliver us from woe; He endured the cross, the dis-
3. On the cross he hung, for the old and young, But he loves the children best; To his arms we'll fly, on his
4. Now ex-alt-ed high, o'er the earth and sky, He delights in mer - cy still, Bends his gracious ear our re-

CHORUS.

God of truth, Let the joy - ful ech - oes fly,
- grace, the loss, Let his praise for - ev - er flow.
grace re - ly And se - cure his prom-ised rest.
- quests to hear, And our long - ing souls to fill.

Sing praises, glad praises,
Sing praises, &c.
Sing praises, &c.
Sing praises, &c.

Sing, children sing, Let your songs arise to the lof-ty skies And ex - ult in God our King.

64 AS FLOWS THE RAPID RIVER.

Words by S. F. Smith. Music by J. R. Osgood.

Prompt.

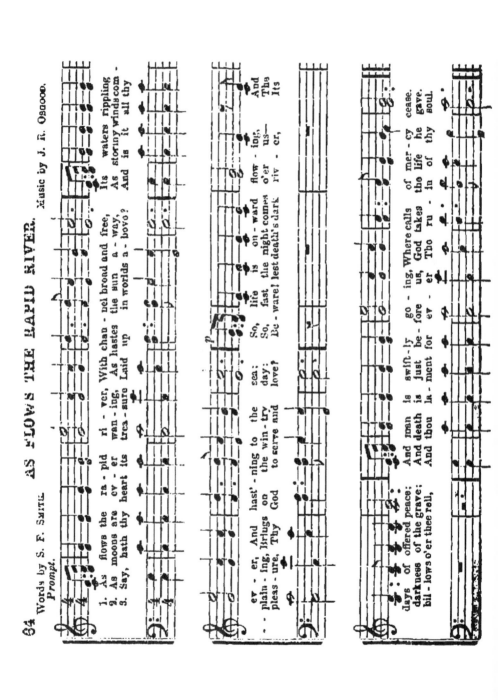

1. As flows the ra - pid ri - ver, With chan - nel broad and free, Its waters rippling
2. As moons are ev - er wan - ing, As hastes the sun a - way, As stormy winds com-
3. Say, hath thy heart its trea - sure Laid up in worlds a - bovo? And is it all thy

ev - er, And hast'-ning to the sea; So, life is on - ward flow - ing, And
- - plain - ing, Brings on the win - try day: So, fast the night comes o'er us— Tha
pleas - ure, Thy God to serve and love? Be - warel lest death's dark riv - er, Its

days of offered peace; And man is swift-ly go - ing, Where calls of mer - cy cease.
darkness of the grave; And death is just be - fore us, God takes the life he gave.
bil - lows o'er thee rell, And thou la - ment for ev - er. Tho ru - in of thy soul

Words by G. W. BUNGAY. AN ANGEL IN THE CLOUD. Music by HENRY TUCKER. 65

Fine.

D. C.

1. { There, sheltered from the wolves and cold, Dear lit - tle lambs with - in the fold, }
{ Are watched with more than shepherd's care, No harm be - falls the weakest there. }
D. C. Rocked on the billows of her breast, Thy sleep emblems thy fu - ture rest.

Sweet dar - ling on thy mother's knee, Sleeping as sleeps a wave at sea;

2. There is an angel in the room,
Whose presence, like the starry bloom
Of heaven, radiates the light,
As though the sun arose at night.
That angel whispered to the child,
And then the little cherub smiled,
It told the sinless babe to fly
To realms of beauty in the sky.

3. The angel vanished, and a cloud
Came with a coffin and a shroud,
But Heaven, reflected in a tear,
Displayed a white wing hovering near.
So let us live that we may all
Find soft wings on our shoulders fall;
There's room enough for all above,
For Heaven is vast as boundless love.

66. THE LESSON OF NATURE

Words by G. W. Bungay. Music by Henry Tucker.

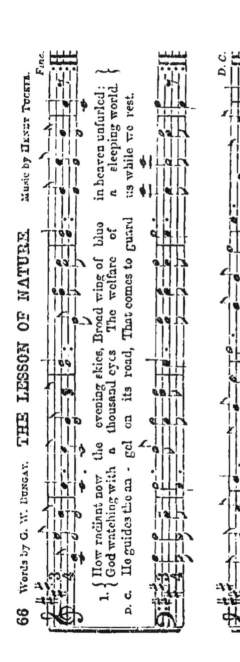

1. { How radiant now the evening skies, Broad wing of blue in heaven unfurled: }
   { God watching with a thousand eyes The welfare of a sleeping world. }

D. C. He guides the an - gel on its road, That comes to guard us while we rest.

He lights the wild flower in the wood, He rocks the spar - row in her nest,

2. When blows the bee his tiny horn,
   To wake the sisterhood of flowers,
   And light shall kindle up the morn.
   Love shall expand these hearts of ours.
   And we will go to Sabbath School,
   And learn the sacred lesson well.
   For stars that shine, and streams that roll,
   Are syllables a child can spell.

3. How sweet the flowers, whose pleasant eyes
   Turn to the sun, as hearts should turn
   To God, whose throne is in the skies,
   Teach us a truth our souls should learn,
   And the loved voices of the birds,
   Fill with soft sounds the listening air,
   As we should turn our thoughts to words,
   In sacred song and simple prayer.

SAY, BROTHERS, WILL YOU MEET US.

From "LEE AVENUE CASKET." By permission.

Arr. by FRANKLIN H. LUNNUS.

1. { *Girls.* Say, brothers, will you meet us, Say, brothers, will you meet us,
{ *Boys.* By the grace of God we'll meet you, By the grace of God we'll meet you,

Full Chor. Glo-ry, glo-ry, hal-le-lu-jah, Glo-ry, glo-ry, hal-le-lu-jah,

Say,... brothers, will you meet us, On Ca-naan's hap-py shore.
By the grace of God we'll meet you, Where part-ing is no more.

Glo-ry, glo-ry, hal-le-lu-jah, For ev - er, ev - er - more.

2.

GIRLS.—Jesus lives and reigns for ever,
Jesus lives and reigns for ever,
Jesus lives and reigns for ever.
On Canaan's happy shore.

BOYS.—Glory, glory, hallelujah,
Glory, glory, hallelujah,
Glory, glory, hallelujah,
For ever, evermore.

Chor. Glory, &c.

68

OH! DO NOT WISH YOUR DARLING BACK.

Music by HENRY TUCKER.

1. Oh, do not wish your dar - ling back To this sad world of care; But rather pray that
3. Yes, safe with - in those pearl - y gates, A - mid the ransomed throng, That infant voice has

those with him E - ter - nal life may share. 2. A gen - tle voice has welcomed him Un -
caught the strain, Joined the an - gel - ic song. 4. Then do not wish your dar - ling back, But
5. All praise to him who gave his Son, Our

to his Saviour's breast; And safe within those lov - ing arms, Your precious treasure* rests.
meek - ly kiss the rod; That lit - tle gem was on - ly lent, It still belonged to God.
dy - ing souls to save, And planted in the Christian's breast, A hope be - yond the grave.

CHILDREN'S PARTING HYMN.*

TUNE—"*Shining Shore*," S. S. BELL, No. 1, p. 104.

1. THE year's last song, and then we part!
How swiftly time is winging!
But sweet are farewells of the heart,
When they are said in singing!
The roses climb the garden wall;
The buds are past their blowing;
The summer's breezy voices call,
And we must now be going!

2. The thrush is on her trembling nest
Which every wind is swaying!
And every robin shows his breast,
While we are here delaying!
The bees have set their pipes in tune
On every head of clover;
And we must haste to hear them soon,
Or summer will be over!

3. To-day the birds on every bough
Their Sabbath chimes are ringing;—
The Lord is in his temple now—
We praise him with our singing!
Without, within, the voices chord!
One praise we all are giving—
To thee, O Ever-loving Lord!
To thee, O Ever-living!

4. O God of every human heart!
And every heart's pure feeling!
We love and praise thee as thou art
In Nature's own revealing!
Wherever summer's grass is green,
Or winter's snows are hoary,
We see thee, though thou art unseen,
We know thee by thy glory!

* This hymn has been sung by the children of the Plymouth Sunday School, on the occasion of their annual closing exercises in the summer, for several years past.

5. We linger in our parting song;
We praise thee as we sever;
The summer days will not be long,
Ere we shall praise for ever!
All hail! then, for the Summer Land
Whose blossoms never wither;
Though here we part each other's hand,
We keep our journey thither!

THEODORE TILTON.

A SUMMER HOLIDAY HYMN.

PIC-NIC SONG.

TUNE—"*Shining Shore*," S. S. BELL, No. 1, p. 104.

1. Now we can bid our books farewell,
And go where winds are blowing
Their flutes of balm in grove and dell,
And gentle doves are cooing.
Away with toil, and dust, and care,
Where toc-sins loud are ringing;
We go to breathe the pleasant air,
Where uncaged birds are singing.

2. The grass lifts up its hands of green,
And waves its flags of clover,
To beckon us to join the scene,
Before the summer's over.
The bobolink perched on his weed,
Like a song-blossom swaying,
Rebukes our steps, and flies with speed,
Where sunshine saves the haying.

3. Wild flower, woodland, and water-fall,
The robin and the roses,
Have given us a tempting call—
But Mammon interposes.
O God of mercy, truth and love,
And ruler of the races,
Stamp with thy seal from heaven above,
All human hearts and faces.

G. W. BUNGAY.

70

THOU, GOD, SEEST ME.

A CHILD'S HYMN.

Words by C. E. K.

Music by Edward Amcell.

4. Whene'er I feel the tempter's power,
   And sin allures my heart from thee,
   May I remember in that hour,
   "Thou, God, seest me."

5. And, Oh, I pray, for Jesus' sake,
   That I a holy child may be,
   And gratefully the message take,
   "Thou, God, seest me."

HAPPY DAYS OF CHILDHOOD. 79.

Words by G. W. Bungay.
Lively. mf

Music by A. Cull.

1. Hap-py, hap-py days of child-hood, Whose glad moments fly like ours— Like the lin-nets in the wild-wood Sing-ing to the sum-mer-showers.

CHORUS.

Is the happy soul, In the Sabbath school, Is the happy soul, In the Sabbath school.

2. Pleasant, pleasant friends and teachers,
In the joyous Sunday school;
Truthful, truthful gospel preachers,
Preaching to the infant soul.
   Chorus—To the infant soul,
    In the Sabbath school,
    To the infant soul,
    In the Sabbath school.

3. Joyful, joyful are the tidings,
Jesus brings to anxious souls;
He will save us from backslidings,
Blessed be the Sabbath schools!
   Chorus—Bless the Sabbath school
    To the infant soul;
    Bless the Sabbath school
    To the infant soul.

72   I OFFER THEE THIS HEART OF MINE.

Words by G. W. Bungay.   Music by L. T. Chadwick.   Arr. by Henry Tucker.

GIVE ME JESUS. Sacred or Revival Hymn.

1. And I heard the mourner say, And I heard the mourner say, Give me Jesus,
2. When I'm happy hear me sing, When I'm happy hear me sing, I have Jesus.
3. O, the judgment day is coming, O, the judgment day is coming, Give me Jesus,

Give me Je-sus, And you may have all the world—Give me Je-sus.
I have Je-sus, And you may have all the world—I have Je-sus.
Give me Je-sus, And you may have all the world—Give me Je-sus.

Give me Je-sus,
I have Je-sus,
Give me Je-sus.

4. Thus I heard a convert sing,
   Thus I heard a convert sing;
   Thus I heard a convert sing,
   I have Jesus, I have Jesus, I have Jesus,
   And you may have all the world—I have Jesus.

5. Oh now hear the voice that calls,
   Oh now hear the voice that calls,
   Oh now hear the voice that calls,
   Come to Jesus, Come to Jesus, Come to Jesus.
   For him give up all the world—Come to Jesus.

6. When the waves of trouble rise,
   When the waves of trouble rise,
   When the waves of trouble rise.
   Give me Jesus, Give me Jesus, Give me Jesus.
   And you may have the world—Give me Jesus.

7. When I languish, worn with pain,
   When I languish, worn with pain,
   When I languish, worn with pain,
   Give me Jesus, Give me Jesus, Give me Jesus,
   And you may have all the world—Give me Jesus

8. When I tread death's valley dark,
   When I tread death's valley dark,
   When I tread death's valley dark,
   Give me Jesus, Give me Jesus, Give me Jesus,
   What then will be all the world ?—Give me Jesus

9. When I reach the spirit land,
   When I reach the spirit land,
   When I reach the spirit land.
   Give me Jesus, Give me Jesus, Give me Jesus,
   For dark would be all that world—Without Jesus

MY SOUL DOTH MAGNIFY THE LORD. Chant.

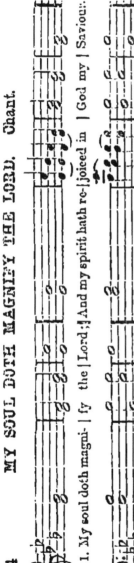
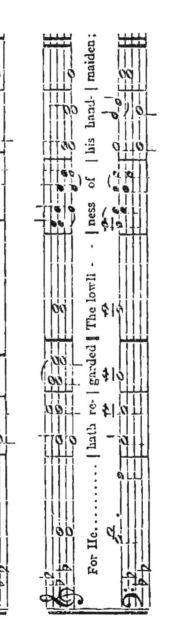

1. My soul doth magni- | fy the | Lord; ‖ And my spirit hath re-|joiced in | God my | Saviour.

For He......... | hath re- | garded | The lowli - - | ness of | his hand- | maiden ;

2. For behold, | from hence- | forth ‖ All gene- | rations · shall | call me | blessed.
For He that is mighty hath magnified me, and holy | is his | Name; ‖ And his mercy is on
them that fear Him, through | all our | gene- | rations.

3. He hath shewed strength | with his | arm ; ‖ He hath scattered the proud in the imagi- | nation
| of their | hearts.
He hath put down the mighty | from their | seats ; ‖ And hath exalted the | humble | and the
| meek.

4. He hath filled the hungry | with good | things ; ‖ And the rich He | hath sent | empty · a- | way.
He remembering his mercy hath holpen his | servant | Israel ; ‖ As He promised to our fore-
fathers, Abraham | and his | seed, for | ever.

THERE IS A LAND MINE EYE HATH SEEN.

Music by J. R. Osgood.

Pia. Flowing.

1. There is a land mine eye hath seen In vis-ions of en-rap-tured tho't, So bright that all which
2. Its skies are not like earth-ly skies, With varying hues of shade and light, It has no need of

lies between, Is with its radiant glo - ry fraught, Is with its ra-diant glo - ry fraught,
suns to rise To dis - si - pate the gloom of night, To dis - si - pate the gloom of night.

3. A land upon whose blissful shore,
   There falls no shadow, rests no stain,
   There those who meet shall part no more,
   And those long parted meet again.
   And those long parted meet again.

4. There sweeps no desolating wind
   Across that calm serene abode;
   The wanderer there a home may find
   Within the Paradise of God.
   Within the Paradise of God.

THOSE EVENING BELLS.

Music by T. Moore, Esq.   Arr. by Henry Tucker.

SOLO or DUET.

1. Those evening bells, those evening bells, How many a tale their music tells,
2. Those joy - ous hours are passed a - way, And many a heart that then was gay,
3. And so 't will be when I am gone, That tune - ful peal will still ring on,

Of youth and home, and that sweet time, When last I heard their soothing chime,
With - in the tomb now dark - ly dwells, And hears no more those eve - ning bells,
While oth - er feet shall walk these dells, And sing your praise, sweet eve - ning bells,

CHORUS.

Of youth and home, and that sweet time, When last I heard their soothing chime.
With - in the tomb now darkly dwells, And hears no more those evening bells.
While oth - er feet shall walk these dells, And sing your praise, sweet evening bells.

RING, SACRED BELLS.

TUNE—"*Those Evening Bells*," p. 76.

1. THOSE sacred bells—those sacred bells,
Their silver tones in music swell,
: Like sweetest voices from that land,
Where children join the angel band. :|

2. Their pleasant tones speak to the soul,
Come early to the Sunday school,
| And when they ring the bosom swells,
With love that chimes with sacred bells. :|

3. Ring out the age of vice and crime,
Ring in the right with holy chime,
Ring in the heart where mercy dwells,
Ring on for ever, sacred bells. |

4. Ring joyous tones in every ear,
Ring loud and let the nations hear;
| Ring in all lands, where virtue dwells,
Bless God for tones from sacred bells. :|

G. W. BUNGAY.

A SONG OF HOPE AND FRIENDSHIP.

TUNE—"*The morning light is breaking*," S. S. Bell, No. 1, p. 96.

1. How sweet when daylight closes,
When sinks the fading sun,
And dew is on the roses,
To meet the dear loved one.
When soft the bells are pealing
Out on the evening air,
And sweetest notes are stealing
Away the sense of care.

2. How sweet when toil is over,
And blossoms close their eyes,
And bees forsake the clover,
And stars look from the skies.
To meet the sweet-faced mother,
And press her gentle hand,
To greet the manly brother,
Or the dear sister bland.

3. How sweet on Sabbath morning,
When toil is hushed and still,
And light from heaven is dawning
On Zion's sacred hill—
To kneel in pure devotion
With the dear ones we love,
When hearts beat with emotion,
Kindled in heaven above.

G. W. BUNGAY.

BANDS OF HOPE.

TUNE—"*Christmas Bells*," p. 95.

1. Bands of Hope are sailing, sailing,
On, right on, before the blast;
Temperance bands are sailing, sailing
Their white banners to the mast.
Speed, speed on the snow-white sail,
Shout to every far-off land;
Hail the temperance ship! all hail!
God speed the temperance bond.
Chorus.—Bands of Hope are sailing, &c.

2. Bands of Hope are forming, forming,
On our free and happy shore;
Bands of Hope are storming, storming,
And their flag is waving o'er
The strong citadel of rum,
Where alcohol held sway;
Now the Bands of Hope have come,
And they shall win the day.
Chorus.—Bands of Hope are forming, &c.

3. Bands of Hope are shouting, shouting,
Here and there, and everywhere,
Flags of Hope are floating, floating
In the sweet and golden air.
Sign the pledge, and join the band,
At the altar and the porch;
March in triumph through the land,
With banner, badge, and torch.
Chorus.—Bands of Hope are shouting, &c.

G. W. BUNGAY.

"KIND SHEPHERD, LEAD ME O'ER THE PLAIN."

Words by Geo. W. Bungay.

Arr. by Henry Tucker.

Little Martha.*

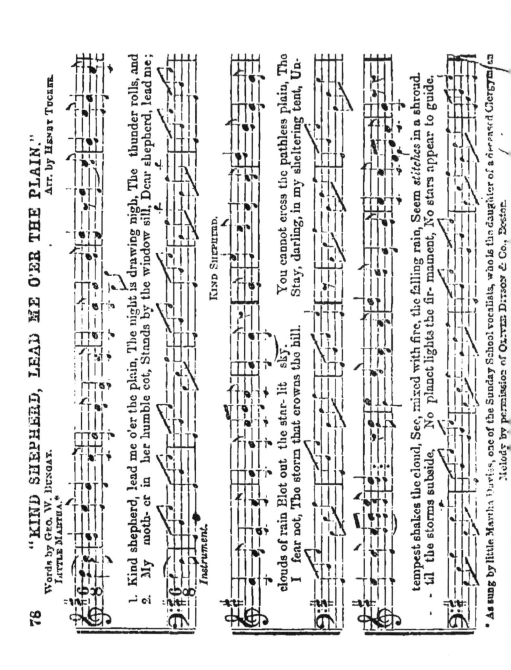

1. Kind shepherd, lead me o'er the plain, The night is drawing nigh, The thunder rolls, and
2. My moth- er in her humble cot, Stands by the window sill, Dear shepherd, lead me;

clouds of rain Blot out the star- lit sky.
I fear not, The storm that crowns the hill.

KIND SHEPHERD.

You cannot cross the pathless plain, The
Stay, darling, in my sheltering tent, Un-

tempest shakes the cloud, See, mixed with fire, the falling rain, Seem *stitches* in a shroud.
- - til the storms subside, No planet lights the fir- mament, No stars appear to guide.

* As sung by little Martha Davis, one of the Sunday School vocalists, who is the daughter of a deceased Clergyman.

Melody by permission of Oliver Ditson & Co., Boston.

"KIND SHEPHERD." (CONCLUDED.)

Chorus by School and Audience.

Kind shepherd, lead her o'er the plain, The night is dark and drear; And

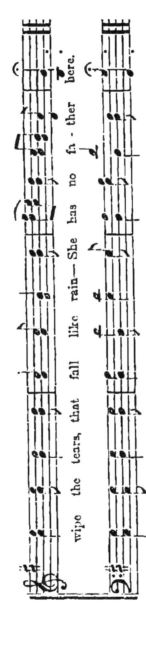

wipe the tears, that fall like rain—She has no fa - ther here.

MARTHA.

3. Oh! shepherd, take me by the hand,
   I see my mother's form,
   She beckons, where the old elms stand,
   An angel in the storm.

   SHEPHERD.

   Thy mother will not meet again,
   Her darling, pleading child,
   If I should lead thee o'er the plain,
   Where winds are howling wild.
   Chorus.—Kind shepherd, &c.

MARTHA.

4. My mother prays for me her child,
   And thunders stop to hear,
   Her accents soft, and sweet, and mild,
   And Jesus bows his ear.

   SHEPHERD.

   Then I will lead thee o'er the plain,
   Through darkness deep and wide,
   The lightning coming with the rain,
   Shall be the lamp to guide.
   Chorus.—Kind shepherd, &c.

HOLY ANGELS, SONS OF GLORY.

Air by R. C. Harmonized by J. Roberts.

1. Ho - ly an - gels, sons of glo - ry, Clothed in robes of light di - vine,

They re - peat the wondrous sto - ry Of a God for sin - ners slain.

CHORUS. *Lively.*

And a - dore the great I Am.

Singing glo - ry, glo - ry, glo - ry,

88

HOLY ANGELS, SONS OF GLORY. (CONCLUDED.)

glo - ry, hal - le - lu - jah, Hal - le - lu - jah to the Lamb, Hal - le - lu - jah to the Lamb.

2.
On their wings of gladness soaring,
Angels do their Lord's behests,
Ever loving and adoring,
Through the regions of the blest;
Thus they swell the heavenly theme:
Singing glory, &c.

3.
Saints and martyrs, faint and weary,
With long wanderings here on earth;
Pilgrims, prophets, aged, hoary,
Heirs of heaven through the new birth;
All exalt the Saviour's name.
Singing glory, &c.

4.
Children, who were meek and lowly,
Followers of their Master here,

5.
Seeking, like him, to be holy,
Now arrayed in beauty there,
Catch the pure seraphic flame,
Singing glory, &c.

5.
Millions more on earth remaining,
Precious lambs of Christ's wide fold,
Who the pearl of price obtaining,
Shall their Jesus' face behold,
And his boundless love proclaim,
Singing glory, &c.

6.
Little children, Christ has bought you,
Bought you with his precious blood;
Give him, then, your hearts and lives, too,
Joined in loving brotherhood,
To extol his blessed name,
Singing glory, &c.

SHOUT THE GLAD TIDINGS.

AVISON.

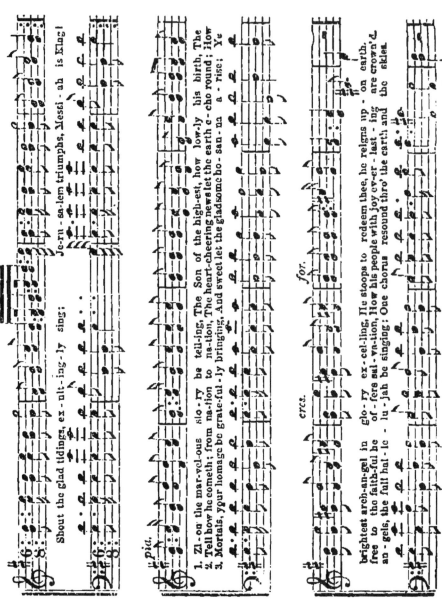

Shout the glad tidings, ex-ult-ing-ly sing; Je-ru - sa-lem triumphs, Messi - ah is King!

1. Zi-on the mar-vel-ous glo-ry be tell-ing, The Son of the high-est, how low-ly his birth, The
2. Tell how he cometh; from na-tion to na-tion, The heart-cheering news let the earth e-cho round; How
3. Mortals, your homage be grate-ful-ly bringing, And sweet let the gladsome ho-san-na a-rise; Ye

brightest arch-an-gel in glo-ry ex-cel-ling, He stoops to redeem thee, he reigns up - on earth.
free to tho faith-ful be of - fers sal - va-tion, How his people with joy ev-er - last - ing are crown'd
an-gels, the full hal-le - lu-jah be singing; One chorus resound thro' the earth and the skies.

SHOUT THE GLAD TIDINGS. (CONCLUDED.)

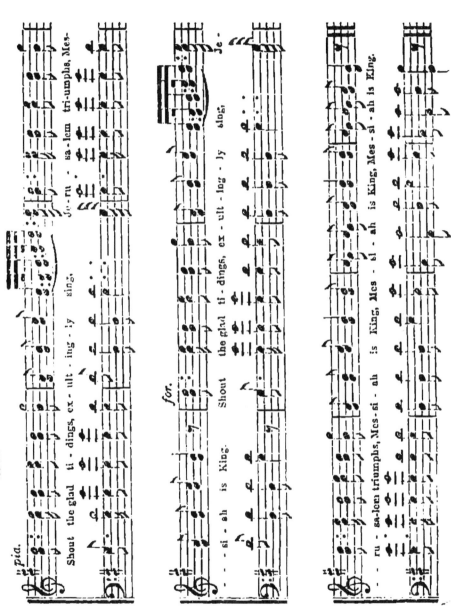

84

SAVIOUR, BREATHE AN EVENING BLESSING.

RUSSIAN AIR.

DUET, or SEMI-CHORUS.

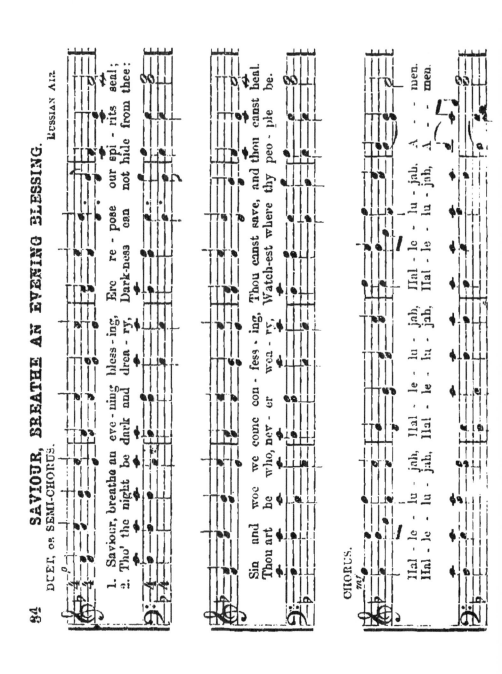

1. Saviour, breathe an eve - ning bless - ing, Ere re - pose our spi - rits seal;
2. Tho' the night be dark and drea - ry, Dark-ness can not hide from thee:

Sin and woe we con - fess - ing, Thou canst save, and thou canst heal.
Thou art he who, nev - er wea - ry, Watch-est where thy peo - ple be.

CHORUS.

Hal - le - lu - jah, Hal - le - lu - jah, Hal - le - lu - jah, A - - - men.
Hal - le - lu - jah, Hal - le - lu - jah, Hal - le - lu - jah, A - - - men.

SAVIOUR, BREATHE AN EVENING BLESSING. (CONCLUDED.)

DUET. *p*

Tho' de-struc-tion walk a - round us, Tho' the ar - rows near us fly,
Should swift death this night o'er-take us, And our couch be - come our tomb.

An - gel guards from thee sur - round us, We are safe, if thou art nigh.
May the morn in heaven a - wake us, Clad in bright and death - less bloom.

CHORUS.
mf

Hal - le - lu - jah, Hal - le - lu - jah, Hal - le - lu - jah, A - - men.
Hal - le - lu - jah, Hal - le - lu - jah, Hal - le - lu - jah, A - - men.

WE LOVE THE HAPPY SCHOOL.

Words by Mrs. M. A. Kidder.   Music by S. C. Foster.   Arranged by A. Cull.

SOLO, or DUET.—*Moderato.*

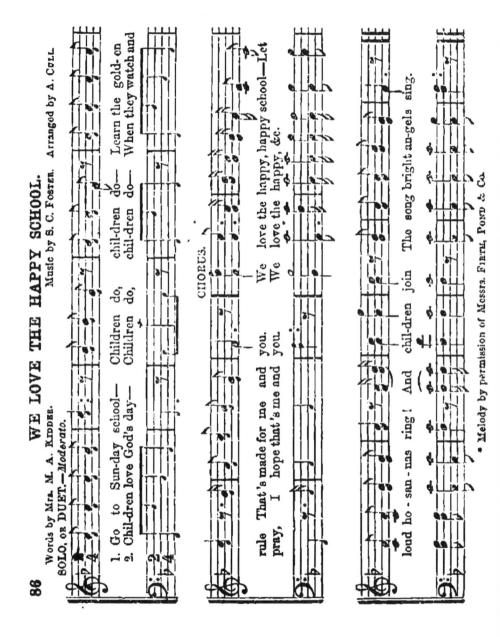

1. Go to Sun-day school— Children do, chil-dren do— Learn the gold-en rule That's made for me and you.
2. Chil-dren love God's day— Children do, chil-dren do— When they watch and pray, I hope that's me and you.

CHORUS.

We love the happy, happy school—Let
We love the happy, &c.

And chil-dren join The song bright an-gels sing.

loud ho - san - nas ring!

* Melody by permission of Messrs. Firth, Pond & Co.

3. Children turn from sin;
   Children do, children do,
   When they're right within;
   I hope that's me and you.
   Chorus—We love, &c.

4. Children fear to lie,
   Children do, children do,
   When their Saviour's nigh;
   I hope that's me and you.
   Chorus—We love, &c.

5. Children feel God's truth;
   Children do, children do,
   Better in their youth;
   I hope that's me and you.
   Chorus—We love, &c.

6. Children wrongs endure;
   Children do, children do,
   When their hearts are pure;
   I hope that's me and you.
   Chorus—We love, &c.

WHAT SOME CHILDREN DO.

TUNE—*"We love the happy School."*

1. SOME vain children try—
   Vain ones do, vain ones do—
   To play the butterfly;
   But not the just and true.
   Chorus—God bless the happy, happy soul,
   That loves the truth and right,
   Loves our Sabbath school,
   And worships God aright.

2. Some bad children swear;
   Bad ones do, bad ones do—
   Never kneel in prayer,
   Not so the just and true.
   Chorus—God bless, &c.

3. Some mean children steal;
   Mean ones do, mean ones do—
   Their hearts do seldom feel,
   As do the just and true.
   Chorus—God bless, &c.

4. Some bad children lie;
   Bad ones do, bad ones do—
   Now let you and I
   Be like the just and true.
   Chorus—God bless, &c.

5. Some bold children fight;
   Bold ones do, bold ones do—
   We know it is not right,
   We will be just and true.
   Chorus—God bless, &c.

6. Some the Sabbath break;
   Bad ones do, bad ones do—
   Now for Jesus' sake
   Let us be just and true.
   Chorus—God bless, &c.

7. Some good children pray—
   Good ones do, good ones do—
   And keep the Sabbath day,
   And they are just and true.
   Chorus—God bless, &c.

8. Some good children love—
   Good ones do, good ones do—
   God who rules above,
   For they are just and true.
   Chorus—God bless, &c.

9. Some good children sing—
   Good ones do, good ones do—
   Christ their Hope and King,
   While they are just and true.
   Chorus—God bless, &c.

G. W. BUNGAY

THE PIC-NIC.

Words and Music by D. E. THOMPSON.

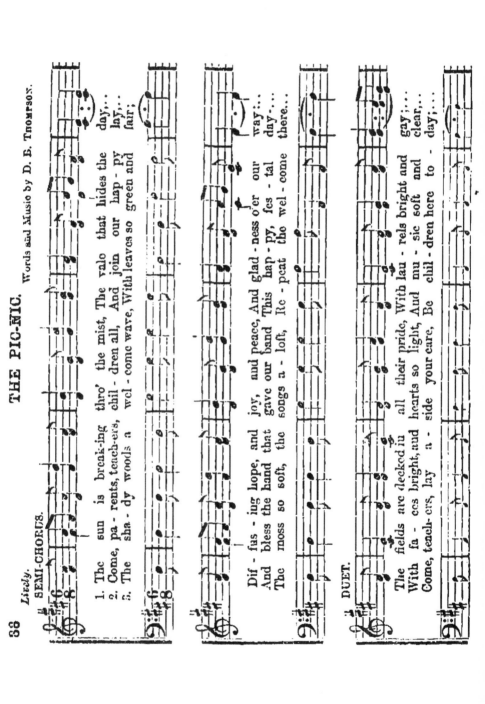

Lively.

SEMI-CHORUS.

1. The sun is break-ing thro' the mist, The vale that hides the day,...
2. Come, pa-rents, teach-ers, chil-dren all, And join our hap-py lay;...
3. The sha-dy woods a wel-come wave, With leaves so green and fair:

Dif-fus-ing hope, and joy, and peace, And glad-ness o'er our way;...
And bless the hand that gave our band This hap-py, fes-tal day-...
The moss so soft, the songs a-loft, Re-peat the wel-come there...

DUET.

The fields are deck-ed in all their pride, With lau-rels bright and gay;...
With fa-ces bright, and hearts so light, And mu-sic soft and clear,...
Come, teach-ers, lay a-side your care, Be chil-dren here to-day;...

THE PIC-NIC. (CONCLUDED.)

Then let us join the mer-ry throng, And to the woods a-way....
This hap-py throng will march a-long, With wav-ing ban-ners cheer...
With speech and song, this joy-ful throng Shall drive dull care a-way....

Rit.

FULL CHORUS TO EACH VERSE.

A-way, a-way, a-way, a-way, Then to the woods a-way,

Then let us join the mer-ry throng, And to the woods a-way.

THE TRY COMPANY.

Music composed expressly for the *Lee Avenue Sunday School Singing Class and Boy's Meeting* by one of their friends,* and arranged by HENRY TUCKER.

1. There is a hope-ful com-pan-y We're just a-bout to start,
And we in-vite you all, young friends, To join us hand and heart
So come and add your name at once, Nor wait till by-and-bye,

THE TRY COMPANY. (CONCLUDED.)

CHORUS.

For 'tis a thing worth join - ing, this— Our com - pa - ny, "The Try."

But in *our* glorious Company
We dare object to none ;

Chorus.

The meanest, dullest, poorest, worst
We've room for every one.

2.

Some Companies there are, you know,
That cost a deal per share,
But all that you need pay for one,
Is—earnestness and prayer ;
And some end so disastrously,
They make folks very cross.

Chorus.

But here you will be sure to gain,
And can not suffer loss ;

3.

And some there are that only crave
The learned or the grand,
And others that alone admit
The wealthiest in the land ;

4.

Then in our brave "Try" Company,
Your every power invest,
For this, whatever others may,
You'll find will pay the best ;
And we will meet another year,
If God our lives should spare.

Chorus.

And we'll promise a good dividend,
To all who take a share,

JESUS, SAVIOUR, AT THY BIDDING. 8s, 7s & 4s.
Words by WILLIAM CUTTER, Esq. Music by E. ROBERTS.

CHORUS.
Oh, the sweetness! oh, the glory!
Far earth's brightest crowns above!
Words can never tell the story
Of our dear Redeemer's love.
   Its full sweetness,
   Its sweet fulness,
All eternity shall prove.

TEACHERS.
To Thy service, Jesus, Saviour,
We these little ones would train;
Smile upon them now with favor,
Let them plead—and not in vain.—
   That the dying,
   That the heathen
May the precious gospel gain.

SCHOLARS.
Hear, O Lord! our supplication,
Thou, whose love has blessed us so—
Let the darkest, lowest nation,
Thy sweet name and gospel know.
   To the children,
   Blessed Saviour,
Everywhere thy goodness show.

CHORUS.
Hear us, mighty Saviour! hear us,
Send thy gospel all abroad!
Let the heathen, far or near us,
Hear, obey, and turn to God.
   Let the Bible,
   Let the Sabbath,
Lighten every dark abode.

* By permission from "WAY DAY WESDAY SCHOOL."

YOUTHFUL DAYS ARE PASSING BY. A Funeral Hymn. 93

Words by R. B.

Music by Miss C. T. Braman. Arr. by A. Cull.

SOLO, or DUET.—*Moderato.*

1. { Youthful days are pass-ing by,   Time is nev - er still,   But the angels
Ma - ny hours and years have fled,   We are chil - dren still,   We are chil-dren
2. { While the Sab-bath-day of rest, Gift from heav-en here,   Leads the low-ly
We will trust in Christ the just, Who loved children here,   Lest the souls in

CHORUS.

hov-er   nigh, Guarding us from ill.... }
with the dead, 'Tis our Father's will.... }
where the blest Shod no mournful tear... }
Sabbath schools Miss the heavenly sphere. }

Like them we too must dwell, resting in the

Like them we too, &c.

dell,   And friends will sigh with tear-wet eye, O'er the dear ones loved so well.

THE RICH EAST INDIAN CHILD.

[A little East Indian girl, who had attended the mission school at Bellary, said, a day or two before her death, "Mother I am going; God bless you!" Her mother rejoined, "My poor child!" She replied, "No, mother; rich, rich; I am going to my Father in heaven."—*London Child's Companion.*]

HENRY TUCKER.

1. { Oh, mo-ther, no: your lit-tle girl Is rich; she is not poor! For her there is a
   { My Fa-ther is the King of kings! And soon to him I go; Then I shall wear a

2. { How hap-py be will make me there, No words of mine can tell; I there shall have no
   { So do not grieve and say, "Poor child!" When in the grave I'm laid: But think how rich with

home in heaven, For her a treasure sure.
beauteous robe, White as the spot-less snow.
want, no sin, But with the an-gels dwell.
God I am, Through that great price he paid.

DUO.

And ne-ver will that gar-ment fade, It
And mo-ther, seek to meet me there, And
And in the ci-ty bright a-Love, At

CHORUS.

de-ver old can be; It is the gift of Him I love, Of him who died for me.
you, my sis-ters dear, So rich and hap-py you will be, When I'm no lon-ger here.
last, a gathered band, We'll ev-er bless our Saviour's name, By whom redeemed we stand.

LIKE GLEAMS OF LIGHT.

Words by Geo. W. Bungar.

Music by Sroar. Arr. by Henry Tucker.

1. Like gleams of light, From stars at night, When sweet flow'rs close their eyes, And bow in prayer, Like
2. The brooklets shout Their welcome out, To ev - cry child they meet; Un-wind-ing rills—From

Fine.

chil-dren there, To God who lights the skies.
spools of hills, In ac - cents low and sweet.

The night - in-gale Wakes hill and dale, Loud
Say, "come, my dears, Wipe dry those tears, The

Rall.- - - - - -

sing - ing as the flies; The light that falls From God's blue walls, Shall lead us to the skies.
sun laughs, so will we. The woods once more, Our songs encore, And clap their leaves in glee.

D. C. Chorus.

BLESSINGS ON THE CHILDREN; or, HARVEST WORK.

Words and Music by J. R. Osgood.

Spirited.

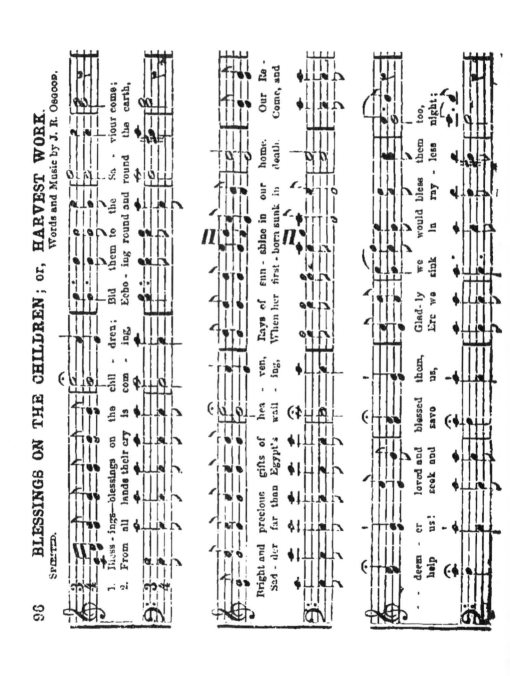

1. Bless - ings - blessings on the chil - dren; Bid them to the Sa - viour come;
2. From all lands their cry is com - ing, Echo - ing round and round the earth,

Bright and precious gifts of hea - ven, Rays of sun - shine in our home.
Sad - der far than Egypt's wail - ing, When her first-born sunk in death.

... er loved and blessed them, Glad-ly we would bless them too, Our Re -
help us! seek and save us, Ere we sink in my - less night; Come, and

BLESSINGS ON THE CHILDREN; or, HARVEST WORK. (Concluded.) 97

"Feed my lambs," is His com - mand - ment, Let us hear and glad - ly do;
Gloom is o'er us! death be - fore us; Send, oh send, the gos - pel's light;
Guide and guard them, Gent-ly lead them Where the "liv - ing wa - ters" flow.
God commands it, Haste to give it, Give the world the Gos - pel's light.

3. Wide the harvest is before thee,
   Bowed the head of golden grain,
   Earnest trust thy gathering sickle
   Ere it falls to earth again.
   Wages—wages God will give thee,
   Better far than monarch's state,
   Earthly grandeur can not treasure,
   Glory, an eternal weight.
      Thus God gives thee—
      Truly gives thee—
      ...ore, an eternal weight.

4. Souls immortal is the harvest,
   All around thee, press they on
   As a heaving, restless ocean
   Up to God's great judgement throne.
   Will ye falter? dare ye dally
   'Mid this countless, deathless throng!
   Up, with all thy powers rally,
   Waits for thee a fadeless crown.
      This thy wages—
      Glorious wages—
      An eternal, fadeless crown

HAPPY SUNDAY SCHOOL;

OR, SABBATH DAYS OF CHILDHOOD'S YEARS.

Words by Geo. W. Bungay. Music by Glover. Arr. by A. Grill.

Allegro Moderato.

1. Sab-bath days of childhood's years, Thy joy and bliss I know; Sun-day school like heaven appears, Where guardian angels bow. My les - son hero un - to me brings, Hope to my heart and soul; The hours are birds on golden wings, In my dear Sunday school; The hours are birds on gold - en wings, The hours are birds on gold - en wings, The hours are birds on gold - en wings, In our hap - py Sun - day school.

HAPPY SUNDAY SCHOOL. (CONCLUDED.)

2.

Pleasant days! how swift their flight!
  How sweet the song we sing!
Starry pinions of the night,
  Why spread thy brooding wing!
The Sabbath day too short appears
  To this young heart of mine.

It lights me through the vale of tears,
  A lamp in hands divine;
It lights me through the vale of tears,
It lights me through the vale of tears,
It lights me through the vale of tears,
  A lamp in hands divine.

Chorus.—Happy school, &c.

100

PLEASANT SABBATH BELL.

Words by Mrs. M. A. Kidder.

Arranged by Henry Tucker.

DUET. *Allegretto.*

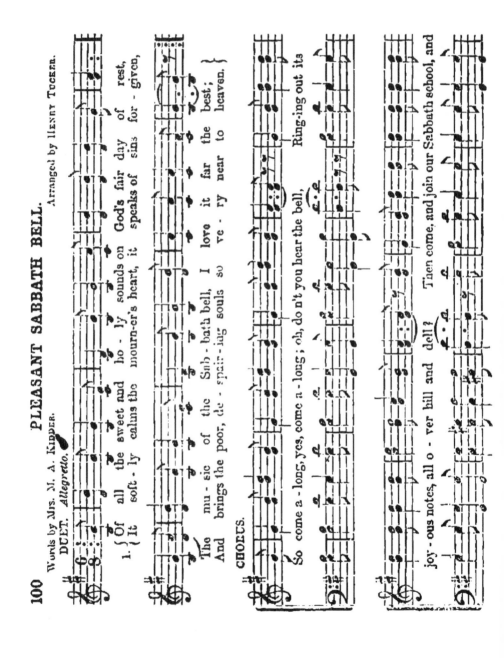

1. $\begin{cases} \text{Of all the sweet and ho - ly sounds on God's fair day of rest,} \\ \text{It soft - ly calms the mourn-er's heart, it speaks of sins for - given,} \end{cases}$

The mu - sic of the Sab - bath bell, I love it far the best;
And brings the poor, de - spair - ing souls so ve - ry near to heaven.

CHORUS.

So come a - long, yes, come a - long; oh, do n't you hear the bell, Ring-ing out its

joy - ous notes, all o - ver hill and dell? Then come, and join our Sabbath school, and

PLEASANT SABBATH BELL. (CONCLUDED.)

make no more de-lay, For when you learn its pleasant rules, you'll never keep a-way.

2.

Every week day brings its cares and troubles to perplex,
And children have their sorrows too, and little things that vex;
But when we hear the Sabbath bells in notes so loud and clear,
We think how wrong it is to fret, when God's so very near.
Chorus.—So come along, &c.

3.

There was a dark benighted time, though many years ago,
When children had no Sabbath schools, where they the truth might know;
And many children now there are, in regions far away,
That never hear the Sabbath bells on God's most holy day.
Chorus.—So come along, &c.

4.

How thankful, then, we'd ought to be, to have one day in seven,
When we can meet our teachers kind, and learn the way to heaven;
What holy thoughts of Jesus should every bosom swell,
As we listen to the music of the blessed Sabbath bell.
Chorus.—So come along, &c.

HEAVEN BLESS THE SCHOOL.

Words by G. W. Bungay. Music by Verdi. Arranged by A. Cull.

DUET.—*Allegretto.*

1. Come to the Sab-bath school, When our glad bells shall toll, Come with a
Like the gay lark on high, Lost in the list-'ning sky, Shall be our

cheer-ful soul, Hap-pi - ly sing - ing. Life like a viv - er flows,
mel - o - dy, Sounding so gay - ly. Rise with the ris - ing sun,

Rude-ly its zephyr blows, Win-ter its mantle throws, Flake on flake fling-ing,
Sing till his race be run, Pray, that God's will be done, Wor-ship him dai - ly,

CHORUS or SOLO.

Fond hearts are beating, Songs we 're repeating, Warm is our greeting, Heaven bless the school.

HEAVEN BLESS THE SCHOOL.　(CONCLUDED.)

103

SOLO SOPRANO.

CHORUS.

104

OUR GLAD VOICES.

Words by Mrs. E. M. Levy.

Scotch Melody. Arr. by HENRY TUCKER.

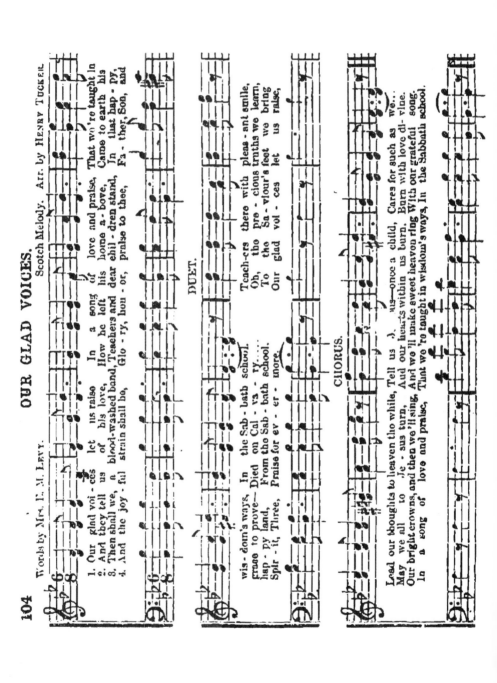

1. Our glad voi - ces let us raise In a song of love and praise, That we're taught in
2. And they tell us of his love, How he left his home a - bove, Came to earth his
3. Then shall we, a blood-washed band, Teachers and dear chil - dren stand, In that hap - py,
4. And the joy - ful strain shall be, Glo - ry, hon - or, praise to thee, Fa - ther, Son, and

DUET.

wis - dom's ways, In the Sab - bath school.
grace to prove— Died on Cal - va - ry.
hap - py land, From the Sab - bath school.
Spir - it, Three, Praise for ev - er - more.

Teach-ers there with pleas - ant smile,
Oh, tho pre - cious truths we learn,
To the Sa - viour's feet we bring
Our glad voi - ces let us raise,

CHORUS.

Lead our thoughts to heaven tho while, Tell us). us once a child, Cares for such as we...
May we all to Je - sus turn, And our hearts within us burn, Barn with love di - vine.
Our bright crowns, and then we'll sing, And we'll make sweet heaven ring With our grateful song.
In a song of love and praise, That we're taught in wisdom's ways, In the Sabbath school.

LOVING KINDNESS. L. M.

1. Awake, my soul, in joyful lays, And sing the great Redeemer's praise; He justly........ns a song from me,

His loving kindness, O how free! His loving kindness, Loving kindness, Loving kindness, His loving kindness, O how free!

2. When trouble, like a gloomy cloud,
Has gathered thick and thundered loud,
He near my soul has always stood,
His loving-kindness, O how good!

3. Often I feel my sinful heart
Prone from my Jesus to depart;
But though I have him oft forgot,
His loving-kindness changes not

4. Soon shall I pass the gloomy vale,
Soon all my mortal powers must fail;
O may my last expiring breath
His loving-kindness sing in death

5. Then let me mount and soar away
To the bright world of endless day;
And sing, with rapture and surprise,
His loving-kindness in the skies.

HURRAH! TO THE WOODS WE GO.

DUET, or QUARTETTE.   A PIC-NIC SONG.   Arranged by HENRY TUCKER.

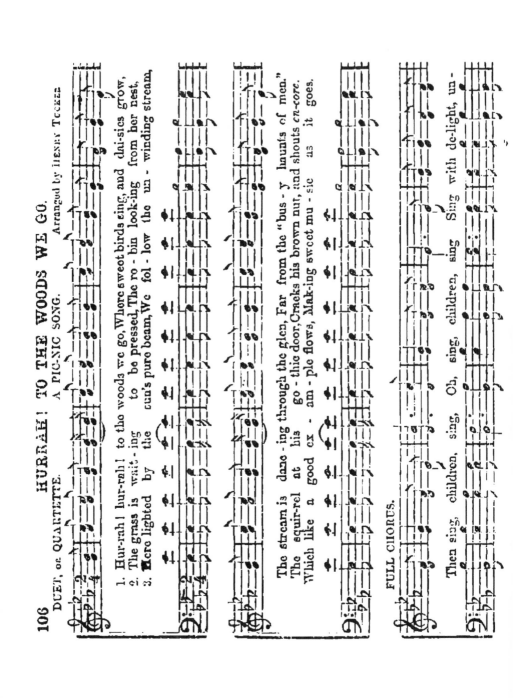

1. Hur-rah! hur-rah! to the woods we go, Where sweet birds sing, and dai-sies grow,
2. The grass is wait-ing to be pressed, The ro-bin look-ing from her nest,
3. Here lighted by the sun's pure beam, We fol-low the un-winding stream,

The stream is danc-ing through the glen, Far from the "bus-y haunts of men."
The squir-rel at his go-thic door, Cracks his brown nut, and shouts en-core.
Which like a good ex-am-ple flows, Mak-ing sweet mu-sic as it goes.

FULL CHORUS.

Then sing, children, sing, Oh, sing, children, sing Sing with de-light, un-

HURRAH! TO THE WOODS WE GO. (CONCLUDED.)

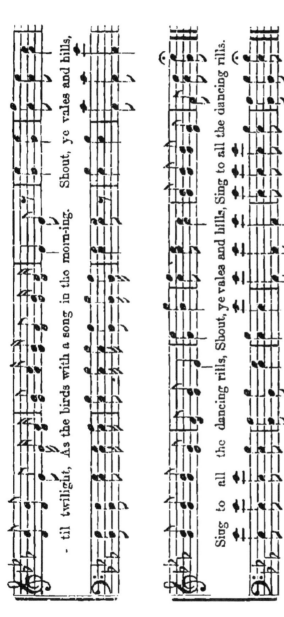

...til twilight, As the birds with a song in the morn-ing. Shout, ye vales and hills,

Sing to all the dancing rills, Shout, ye vales and hills, Sing to all the dancing rills.

Chorus.—Then sing, &c.

4.

The trees seem bending with their birds,
To cheer us with their pleasant words,
Sweet words dissolving into song,
To cheer and charm this happy throng.
Chorus.—Then sing, &c.

5.

Hurrah, hurrah for happy hours,
In woodlands with the birds and flowers,
Where nature wears a smiling brow,
And joy, like her clear streamlets, flow.
Chorus.—Then sing, &c.

G. W. BUNGAY.

WE, A BAND OF HAPPY CHILDREN.

Words and Music by C. HATCH SMITH, A M

Allegro.

1. { We, a band of hap-py chil-dren, Here will meet one day in sev - en;
   { Meet to learn the pre-cious Bi - ble— Gos - pel news of Christ in heav-en.

Aid - ed by our faith-ful teach-ers, Con - stant prayer and praise we'll blend,

With the an - gel hosts, re - joic - ing Now with Christ, the chil-dren's Friend

WE, A BAND OF HAPPY CHILDREN. (CONCLUDED.)

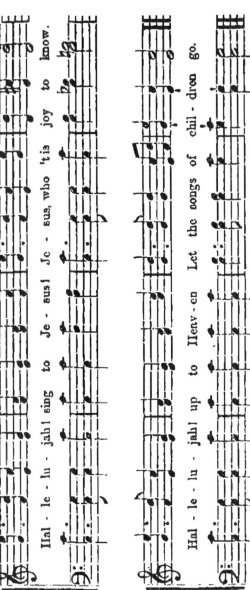

CHORUS.

Hal - le - lu - jah! sing to Je - sus! Je - sus, who 'tis joy to know.

Hal - le - lu - jah! up to Heav - en Let the songs of chil - dren go.

2. Suffer such to come, said Jesus,
   When, on earth, he took a child
   In His holy arms to bless it—
   God—divine—by man reviled.
   On the cross, He died to save us,
   Opening wide the Heav'nly door;
   Asking all to enter through it,
   There to praise him evermore.

   Hallelujah, &c.

3. Praise to Jesus! let us children
   Sing together, how his name
   Carries joy to all the nations—
   Life eternal—heavenly fame.
   Such the news we learn of Jesus,
   He, who is the children's Friend;
   Angel bands, our chorus joining,
   Further up the strain will send.

   Hallelujah, &c.

110

THE DEWY ROSE OF SHARON.

Words by Mrs. M. A. Kidder. Music by Harroway. Arr. by A Cull.

DUET.—*Andante.*

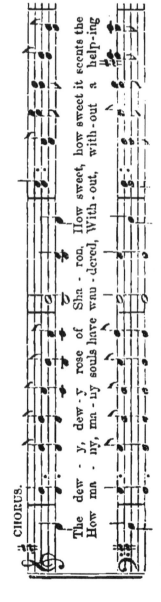

1. The dew - y, dewy rose of Sha - ron, How sweet, how sweet it scents the air, A
2. How ma - ny, many souls have wandered, With-out, with-out a help-ing hand; Their

crown, a crown of matchless glo - ry Up - on its fore-head fair! So we in deeds of
light, their light and beauty fad - ed, Their bark up-on the strand; When one small act of

goodness Un - til our life shall close, May scatter bloom and fragrance Like Sharon's dewy rose.
kindness, One lit-tle look of love, Might add another jew - el To Je - sus' crown a-bove.

CHORUS.

The dew - y, dew - y rose of Sha - ron, How sweet, how sweet it scents the
How ma - ny, ma - ny souls have wan - dered, With - out, with - out a help - ing

air. A crown, a crown of matchless glo-ry Up-on its fore-head fair.
band; Their light, their light and beau-ty fad-ed, Their bark up-on the strand

3. Oh! may we, may we, erring children,
 Though few, though few our talents be,
 A band, a band of young disciples,
 Our Saviour's footprints see;
 And may we humbly follow,
 Till life's uncertain close,
 And leave in death a fragrance
 Like Sharon's dewy rose.
 Chorus.—Oh! may we, &c.

MY MOTHER DEAR!

TUNE—"*The dewy Rose of Sharon.*"

1. My mother dear! my mother dear!
 How oft, how oft! I think of thee,
 While weeks and months roll o'er me here
 Where duty bids me be.
 My mother dear—how sweet the name,
 When thinking o'er the past!
 A mother's love is e'er the same—
 It beats on till the last.
 Chorus. My mother dear! my mother, &c.

2. My mother dear, it grieves me now,
 To think, to think, how oft your son
 Hath grieved your aching heart and brow
 When in sin's paths he run.
 My mother dear, those days of youth,
 Now long since past and gone,
 Left many a seed of holy truth,
 Which since, we hope, have grown.
 Chorus. My mother dear, it grieves, &c.

3. My mother dear, my fervent prayer,
 Is that, is that you may be blest,
 With peace and joy while ling'ring here—
 Foretastes of future rest.
 And that we all may meet at last
 In yonder heavenly sphere,
 At Jesus' feet our crowns to cast—
 All saved, my mother dear.
 Chorus. My mother dear, my fervent, &c.

T. S.

HARK! THE HERALD ANGELS SING.

TELEMANN'S CHANT.

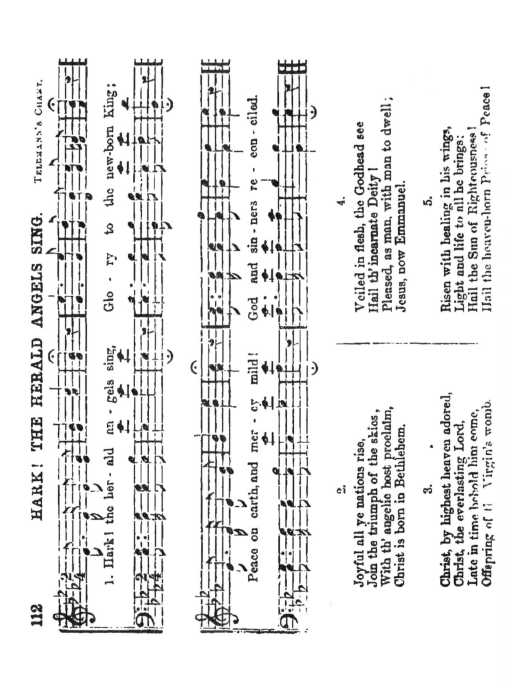

1. Hark! the her - ald an - gels sing,
Glo - ry to the new-born King;

Peace on earth, and mer - cy mild!
God and sin - ners re - con - ciled.

2.

Joyful all ye nations rise,
Join the triumph of the skies,
With th' angelic host proclaim,
Christ is born in Bethlehem.

3.

Christ, by highest heaven adored,
Christ, the everlasting Lord,
Late in time behold him come,
Offspring of the Virgin's womb.

4.

Veiled in flesh, the Godhead see
Hail th' incarnate Deity!
Pleased, as man, with man to dwell;
Jesus, now Emmanuel.

5.

Risen with healing in his wings,
Light and life to all he brings;
Hail the Sun of Righteousness!
Hail the heaven-born Prince of Peace!

STRIKE THE CYMBAL.

Music by PICOTTE. Arr. by HENRY TUCKER.

113

SOLO. Soprano.

{ Strike the cymbal, roll the tymbal, Let the trump of triumph sound;
{ From the riv-er, re-ject-ing quiver, Ju-dah's he-ro takes the stone.

CHORUS.

Powerful slinging! Head-long bringing Proud Go-li-ath to the ground.
Spread your banners! Shout ho-sannas! Bat-tle is the Lord's a-lone.

BOY'S SOLO. Alto.

See ad-vances, with songs and dances,
{ All the band of Is-rael's daughters;
{ Catch the sound, ye hills and waters,

STRIKE THE CYMBAL. (CONTINUED.)

114

STRIKE THE CYMBAL. (CONCLUDED.)

116

THE TEACHER'S APPEAL.

Words by G. W. Bungay.
Bavarian Melody. Arr. by Henry Tucker.

SOLO, or DUET.

1. Like riv-ers swift flow-ing to - ward the deep o - cean, Past isl - ands and meadows so green and so fair, Our life - tides are pulse-ing us on with e -

CHORUS.

- mo - tion, To glo - ry and beau - ty we soon shall be there. Shall we

meet? Shall we meet? In glo - ry and beau-ty we soon shall be there.

2. Dear children, our labors of love are the token
We offer the Saviour, who died for us here,
Whose body was mangled, whose great heart was broken,
With pity for teachers and children so dear.
Jesus died,
With pity for teachers and children so dear.

3. Fond parents, whose bosoms with love over-welling,
For dear ones in Sabbath school classes that meet,
Join anthems of rapture the angels are swelling,
While nations the chorus of children repeat.
Songs so sweet—songs so sweet,
While nations the chorus of children repeat.

4. The song-birds are singing so flute-like their praises,
Now winging o'er woodland, and island, and glen,
To soft notes in meadows, all covered with daisies,
Let us be all cheerful in Sabbath school then.
Let all men—let all men,
Let us be all cheerful in Sabbath school then.

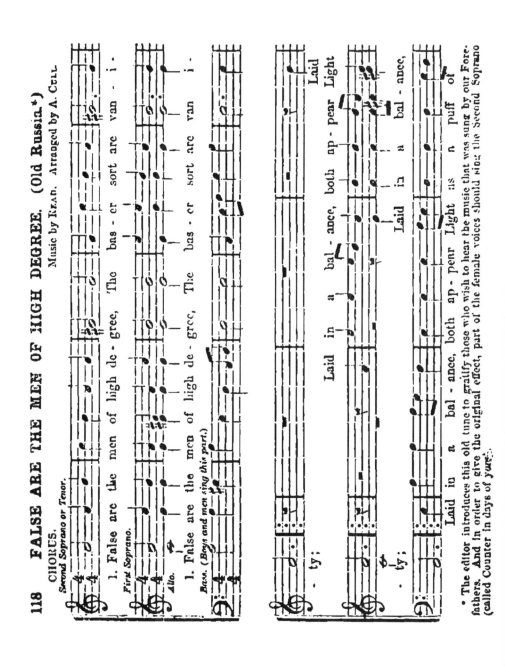

118 FALSE ARE THE MEN OF HIGH DEGREE. (Old Russia.*)

Music by KEAD. Arranged by A. CELL.

CHORUS.

* The editor introduces this old tune to gratify those who wish to hear the music that was sung by our Fore-fathers. And in order to give the original effect, part of the female voices should sing the Second Soprano (called Counter in days of yore).

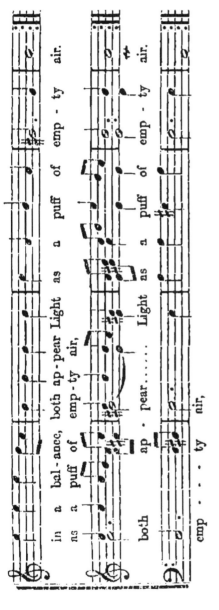

in a bal-ance, both ap-pear Light as a puff of emp - ty air.

as a puff of emp-ty air,

both ap-pear...... Light as a puff of emp - ty air.

emp - - - ty air,

2.
Make not increasing gold your trust,
Nor set your hearts on glittering dust:
Why will you grasp the fleeting smoke,
And not believe what God has spoke!

3.
Once has his awful voice declared,
Once and again my ears have heard:
"All power is his eternal due;
He must be feared and trusted, too."

3.
For sovereign power reigns not alone,
Grace is a partner of the throne:
Thy grace and justice, mighty Lord,
Shall well divide our last reward

WHAT ARE THOSE SOUL-REVIVING STRAINS?

1. What are those soul-reviving strains
Which echo thus from Salem's plains;
What anthems loud, and louder still,
So sweetly sound from Zion's hill?

2. Lo! 'tis an infant chorus sings
Hosanna to the King of kings:
The Saviour comes!—and babes proclaim
Salvation, sent in Jesus' name.

3. Proclaim hosannas loud and clear;
See David's Son and Lord appear!
All praise on earth to him be given,
And glory shout through highest heaven

120

THE GERMAN WATCHMAN'S SONG.*

Music by HEFFERNAN.   Arr. by HENRY TUCKER.

QUARTETTE.

1. Hark! ye neighbors, and hear me tell,   Ten now strikes on the night - ly bell;

DUET.

Ten are the ho - ly commandments given   To man be - low   from God in heaven.

QUARTETTE.

DUET.

Hu - man watch from harm can't ward us,   God will watch, and God will guard us,

* Among the watchmen in Germany, a custom prevails of singing devotional hymns as well as songs of a national or amusing character. The several stanzas of this piece are sung as the hours of the night are successively announced.

CHORUS,

He, through his o - ter - nal night, Grant us all a bless - ed night.

2.

Hark! ye neighbors, and hear me tell,
Eleven sounds on the nightly bell;
Eleven Apostles of holy mind
Taught the Gospel to mankind.
Chorus.—Human watch, &c.

3.

Hark! ye neighbors, and hear me tell,
Twelve resounds from the nightly bell;
Twelve Disciples to Jesus came,
Who suffered rebuke for the Saviour's name.
Chorus.—Human watch, &c.

4.

Hark! ye neighbors, and hear me tell,
One has pealed on the nightly bell,

One God above, one Lord indeed,
Who bears us up in hour of need.
Chorus.—Human watch, &c.

5.

Hark! ye neighbors, and hear me tell,
Two now rings from the nightly bell;
Two paths before mankind are free:
Neighbor, oh! choose the best for thee.
Chorus.—Human watch, &c.

6.

Hark! ye neighbors, and hear me tell,
Three now sounds on the nightly bell;
Threefold reigns the heavenly host,
Father, Son, and Holy Ghost.
Chorus.—Human watch, &c.

WE'LL THANK HIM.

Words and Music by E. S. Taylor.

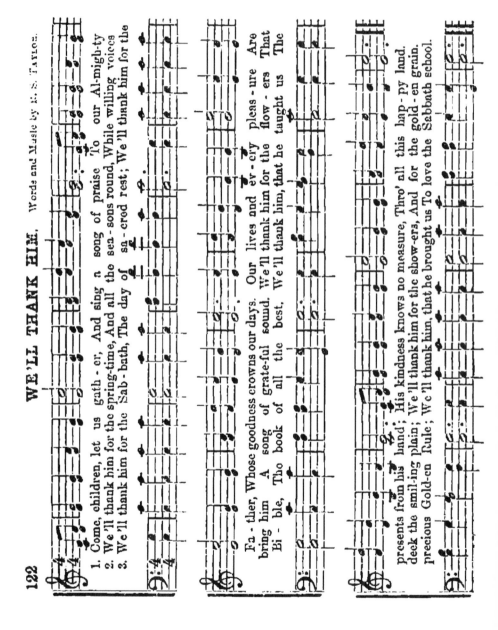

1. Come, children, let us gath - er, And sing a song of praise To our Al-migh-ty
2. We'll thank him for the spring-time, And all the sea-sons round, While willing voices
3. We'll thank him for the Sab - bath, The day of sa - cred rest; We'll thank him for the

Fa - ther, Whose goodness crowns our days. Our lives and ev - ery pleas - ure Are
bring him A song of grate-ful sound. We'll thank him for the flow - ers That
Bi - ble, Tho book of all the best. We'll thank him, that he taught us The

presents from his hand; His kindness knows no measure, Thro' all this hap-py land.
deck the smil-ing plain; We'll thank him for the show-ers, And for the gold-en grain.
precious Gold-en Rule; We'll thank him, that he brought us To love the Sabbath school.

TWINKLE, TWINKLE, LITTLE STAR.

Arranged by HENRY TUCKER.

1. Twinkle, twinkle, lit-tle star, How I wonder what you are, Up above the world so high,

Like a diamond in the sky, Twinkle, twinkle, lit-tle star, How I wonder what you are.

2. When the glorious sun is set,
When the grass with dew is wet,
There you show your little light,
Twinkle, twinkle all the night.
Twinkle, twinkle, &c.

3. In the dark blue sky you keep,
And often through my curtains peep !
For you never shut your eye
Till the sun is in the sky.
Twinkle, twinkle, &c.

4. As yon bright and tiny spark
Lights the traveler in the dark,
Though I know not what you are,
Twinkle, twinkle, little star.
Twinkle, twinkle, &c.

"I MUST BE A LOVING CHILD."

1. I must be a loving child,
Gentle, patient, meek, and mild;
Must be honest, simple, true,
In my words and actions, too ;

I must cheerfully obey,
Giving up my will and way;

2. Must not always thinking be
What is pleasantest to me,
But must try kind things to do,
And make others happy, too.
And in all I do or say,
In my lessons, or my play,

3. Must remember God can view
All I think, and all I do;
Glad that he can know I try,
Glad that children such as I,
In our feeble ways and small,
Can serve him who loves us all

"IN THE SUN, THE MOON, THE SKY."

In the sun, the moon, the sky;
On the mountains wild and high;
In the thunder, in the rain,
In the grove, the wood, the plain;
In the little birds who sing—
God is seen in every thing,

THE OLD FASHIONED BIBLE.

Scotch Melody.   Arr. by HENRY TUCKER.

CHORUS.

124

1. How pain-ful-ly pleasing the fond re-col-lec-tion   Of youthful e-mo-tions and in - no-cent joy,
2. That Bi-ble, the vol-ume of God's in-spi-ra-tion,   At morn and at evening could yield us delight;
3. Ye scenes of tran-quil-li-ty, long have we parted;   My hopes almost gone, and my parents no more;

When blest with pa - ren - tal   ad - vice and af - fec - tion,   Sur - round-ed with mer - cies, with
The prayer of our sire   was   a   sweet in - vo - ca - tion   For mer - cy   by day, and for
In sor - row and sad - ness I   live bro-ken - heart-ed,   And wan-der   un-known on   a

peace from on high,   I   still view the chairs of   my sire and   my mother,   The
safe - ty   thro' night.   Our hymns of thanks-giv-ing,   with har - mo - ny   swelling,   All
far - dis - tant shore.   Yet how can I doubt a   dear Sa-viour's pro - tec - tion,   For -

THE OLD FASHIONED BIBLE. Concluded.

CHORUS.

seats of their off-spring, as ranged on each hand;   And that rich-est book, which ex-
warm from the hearts of a fam-i-ly hand,   Half raised us from earth to that
- - -get-ful of gifts from his boun-ti-ful hand;   Oh, let me with pa-tience re -

cels ev-ery oth-er,   The Fam-i-ly Bi-ble   which lay on the stand;   The
rap-tur-ous dwelling,   De-scribed in the Bi-ble   that lay on the stand;   The
- - ceive his cor-rec-tion,   And think of the Bi-ble   that lay on the stand;   The

old fashioned Bi-ble, The dear, blessed Bi-ble, The Fam-i-ly Bi-ble that lay on the stand.
old fashioned Bi-ble, &c.

126

STAR OF THE MORNING.

DUET AND CHORUS.

Words by Miss C.

Music by Henry Tucker.

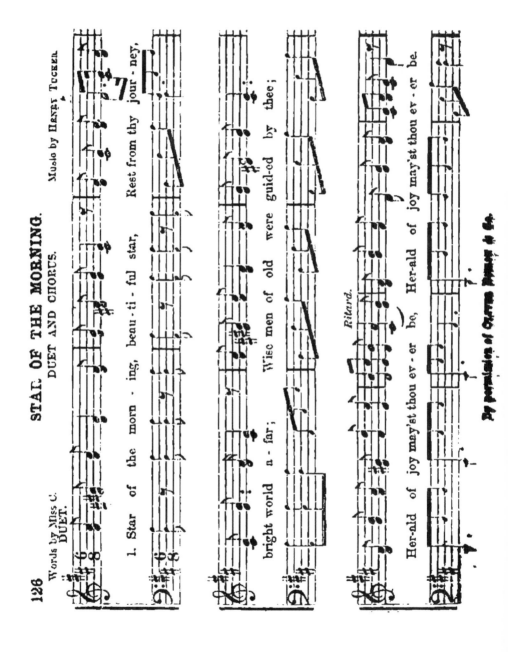

STAR OF THE MORNING. (CONCLUDED.)

2. Lone in thy glory, trembling star,
Tell us thy mission, what joys there are,
Something of life seems moving thee now,
Beings of glory, radiant as thou,
Beings of glory, radiant as thou
Chorus.—Beautiful star, &c.

3. Goddess of beauty, dazzling star,
Tipping with silver the sky gates afar,
Like a lost diamond gleams through the blue
Cloudlets where sunlight is glimmering, too,
Gleams through where sunlight is glimmering, [too.
Chorus.—Beautiful star, &c.

128

EARLY LOST, EARLY SAVED.

Words by G. W. Bethune, D. D.

Scotch Air.　Arr. by Henry Tucker.

CHORUS.

1. With - in her downy cradle, there lay a lit - tle child, And a group of hovering an-gels un -
2. One breathed upon her features, and the babe in beauty grew, With a cheek like morning's blushes, and an
3. An - oth - er gave her accents, and a voice as mu-sic - al As a spring bird's joyous carol, or a

DUET.

seen up-on her smiled; When a strife a - rose among them, a lov-ing, ho - ly strife, Which should
eye of a - zure hue; Till.... ev-ery one who saw her was thankful for the sight Or a
rippling streamlet's fall; Till.... all who heard her laughing, or her words of childish grace, Loved as

CHORUS.

shed the richest blessing up - on her newbo-rn fe. When a strife a - rose a-mong them, a
face so sweet and radiant with ev - er fresh de - light. Till.... ev - ery one who saw her was
much to listen to her,... as to look up - on her face Till.... all who heard her laughing, or her

lov-ing, ho - ly strife, Which should shed the rich-est blessing up - on the new-born life.
thankful for the sight Of a face so sweet and ra - diant with ev - er fresh de - light.
words of child-ish grace, Loved us much to lis-ten to her, as to look up-on her face.

4. Another brought from heaven a clear and gentle mind,
   And within the lovely casket the precious gem enshrined;
   Till all who knew her wondered that God should be so good
   As to bless with such a spirit a world so cold and rude.

5. Thus did she grow in beauty, in melody and truth,
   The budding of her childhood just opening into youth;
   And to our hearts yet dearer, every moment than before,
   She became, though we thought fondly heart could not love her more.

6. Then out spake another angel, nobler, brighter than the rest,
   As with strong arm, but tender, he caught her to his breast:
   "Ye have made her all too lovely for a child of mortal race,
   But no shade of human sorrow shall darken o'er her face:

7. "Ye have tuned to gladness only the accents of her tongue,
   And no wail of human anguish shall from her lips be wrung;
   Nor shall the soul that shineth so purely from within
   Her form of earth-born frailty, ever know a sense of sin.

8. "Lulled in my faithful bosom, I will bear her far away,
   Where there is no sin, nor anguish, nor sorrow, nor decay;
   And mine a boon more glorious than all your gifts shall be—
   Lo! I crown her happy spirit with immortality!"

138

MERRILY THE TEMPERANCE HORN.

Music by J. H. Hewitt. Arr. by Harry Thomas.

DUET.—*Allegretto.*

1. Mer-ri-ly the temp'rance horn Is sounding o'er the ril-ver lake,

Cheer-i-ly at ear-ly dawn Its swell-ing notes bid ech-o wake.

CHORUS.

Temp'rance, for thee, thee on ly   These sounds are ev-er sweet to

me,... Each haunt of pleasure lone-ly   Is found when 'tis un-blest by

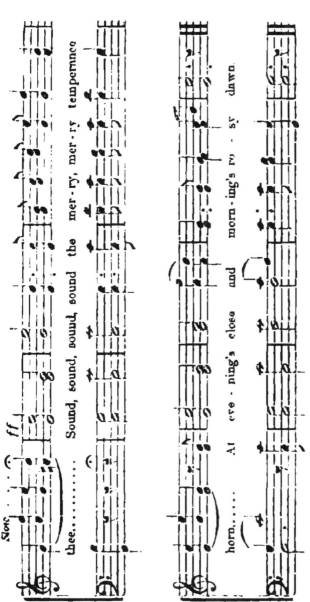

MERRILY THE TEMPERANCE HORN. (CONCLUDED.)

Slow.

ff

thee........ Sound, sound, sound the mer-ry, mer-ry temperance

horn........ At eve-ning's close and morn-ing's ro - sy dawn

2.

Cheerfully my harp I bring,
And wake a wilder, sweeter strain,
Joyously my song I sing,
And bid th' inebriate smile again
Chorus.—Temperance, for thee, &c.

3.

Cheerily our footsteps stray,
Nor wait to think of danger near;
Merrily, at close of day,
We breathe the sweetest music here
Chorus.—Temperance, for thee, &c.

132 LETTERS OF MADGIE TO HER TWIN SISTER, MINNIE, DECEASED.

ANDANTE.

Words from *The Presbyterian.* Music arr. by A. CULL.

1. Min-nie! Minnie! dear-est sis-ter! Whither have you gone from me? Tell me—have you
2. O! then, shall I no more see you? Will you not come back to me? Will you always

gone to heaven, Lit-tle an-gel there to be? Mother, sis-ter, all as-sure me
live with Je-sus, Lit-tle an-gel al-ways be? Do you love to live with Je-sus,

That you're up in heaven now, That you're gone to be with Jesus, Tell me, Min-nie, is it so?
In your new and heavenly home? Does he love all little children? Does he say they all may come?

GOD IS MY FRIEND.

TUNE—Hebron.

1. God is my friend; I need not fear,
For he is good, and always near,
And he will keep me by his power,
From day to day, from hour to hour.

2. I am a sinner—but I know—
For God's own Word has told me so—
That Jesus Christ came down from heaven,
To die that I might be forgiven.

3. There is one thing that I must dread,
And that is Sin; for God has said,
That those whom he protects from ill,
Must love to do his holy will.

ROUSE YE AT THE SAVIOUR'S CALL.

TUNE—"Our glad voices," S. S. Bell, No. 2, p. 104.

1. Rouse ye at the Saviour's call!
Children, rouse ye one and all;
Wake, or soon your souls will fall,
Fall in deep despair.
Woe to him who turns away,
Jesus kindly calls to-day;
Come, O children, while you may,
Raise your souls in prayer.

2. Heard ye not the Saviour cry,
"Turn, O turn, why will ye die!"
And in keenest agony,
Mourn too late your doom!
Haste, for time is rushing on!
Soon the fleeting hour is gone,
The lifted arrow flies anon,
To sink you in the tomb.

3. By the Saviour's bleeding love,
By the joys of heaven above,
Let these words your spirits move;
Quick to Jesus fly!
Come, and save your souls from death,
Haste! escape Jehovah's wrath,
Fly! for life's a fleeting breath,
Soon, O soon you'll die.

---

3. Are you happy up in heaven?
Is your home a pleasant place?
Do they love you there as I do?
Tell me, Minnie, O, do tell me
What I wish so much to know—
How you love your home in heaven,
Where, they say, good children go.

4. Tell me, in my midnight slumbers,
When I dream that you have come;
You can then so sweetly tell me
All about your heavenly home.
When I'm sleeping, some bright angel
Stands beside me all the while;
Is it you, my dearest Minnie,
Bending o'er me with that smile?

5. Then you'll surely tell me, Minnie,
For I want to go there, too,
If Jesus calls me; 't will be heaven
To live and love with him and you!
You have gone to heaven before me;
I must wait the Saviour's will;
If years I tarry, will you, Minnie,
Be a little angel still?

6. If you're a little angel always,
I shall know you when I go;
Do they call you "Minnie" up there—
Will they call me "Madgie," too?
Can you not come back, sweet Minnie?
To keep you, do they love you so?
Must you always live with Jesus?
Then I want to live there, too!

7. We oped our eyes on life together,
But yours were first to close in death;
And yet—O! soon may Madgie greet you,
For life is fleeting as a breath!
How sweet 't will be when father, mother,
Brothers, sisters, mourn no more,
But meet in heaven with "Little Minnie,"
Who is "not lost, but gone before!"

134

BY-AND-BYE.

Arranged by Henry Tucker.

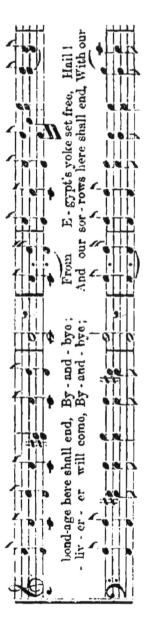
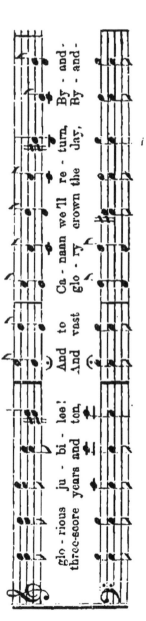

1. Our bond-age here shall end, By - and - bye, by - and - bye; Our
2. Our De - liv - er - er will come, By - and - bye, by - and - bye; Our De-

bond-age here shall end, By - and - bye; From E - gypt's yoke set free, Hail!
- liv - er - er will come, By - and - bye; And our sor-rows here shall end, With our

glo - rious ju - bi - lee! And to Ca - naan we'll re - turn, By - and-
three-score years and ten, And vast glo - ry crown the day, By - and-

BY-AND-BYE. (CONCLUDED.)

135

- bye, by - and - bye. And to Ca - naan we'll re - turn, By - and - bye.
- bye, by - and - bye. And vast glo - ry crown the day, By - and - bye.

3. Though our enemies are strong,
    We'll go on, we'll go on,
   Though our enemies are strong,
    We'll go on.
   Tho' our hearts dissolve with fear,
    Lo! Sinai's God is near,
   While the fiery pillar moves,
    We'll go on, we'll go on, &c.

4. By Marah's bitter stream,
    We'll go on, we'll go on.
   By Marah's bitter stream,
    We'll go on.
   Though Baca's vale be dry,
    And the land yield no supply.
   To a land of corn and wine,
    We'll go on, we'll go on, &c.

5. And when to Jordan's flood,
    We are come, we are come,
   And, when to Jordan's flood,
    We are come.

   Jehovah rules the tide,
    And the waters he'll divide,
   And the ransomed host shall shout,
    We are come, we are come, &c.

6. There friends shall meet again,
    Who have loved, who have loved.
   There friends shall meet again,
    Who have loved.
   Our embraces shall be sweet,
    At the dear Redeemer's feet,
   When we meet to part no more,
    Who have loved, who have loved, &c

7. Then, with all the happy throng,
    We'll rejoice, we'll rejoice,
   Then, with all the happy throng,
    We'll rejoice.
   Shouting, "Glory to our King,"
    Till the vaults of heaven shall ring,
   And through all eternity,
    We'll rejoice, we'll rejoice, &c.

THERE'S WORK ENOUGH FOR ALL.

Words and Music by E. S. TAYLOR.

1. { There's work e - nough, there's work e - nough, And work that should be done, }
   { For lit - tle heads and lit - tle hands—E - nough for ev - ery one. }

2. { In ev - ery place are boys and girls, That nev - er go to school, }
   { Who nev - er hear the Bi - ble read, Nor learn the Gold - en Rule. }

CHORUS.

Then join our throng, and join our song; O - bey the Saviour's call; There's ea-sy work and

pleas - ant work, And work e - nough for all. Work e - nough for all..... Work

THERE'S WORK ENOUGH FOR ALL. (CONCLUDED.)

ALL.

work e - nough for all Here's en - sy work and pleasant work, And work enough for all.

2. There the truths of inspiration,
   Being read with admiration,
   And with souls of adoration,
   In our blest Sabbath school.
     We're a band, &c.

3. There the words of life are learning,
   And our youthful hearts are burning
   With Christ's love, to whom we're turning,
   In the blest Sabbath school.
     We're a band, &c.

4. Yes, the prospect is most cheering,
   And the children most endearing,
   When we see them heavenward steering,
   In the blest Sabbath school.
     With our band of teachers,
     With our band of teachers,
     With our band of teachers,
       And with parents at their side.

3. Those boys and girls we can seek out,
   And take them by the hand,
   And plead with them to come with us,
   To join our happy band.—*Chorus.*

4. Then let us all unite in this,
   And make it for a rule,
   That we will each do all we can,
   To help the Sabbath school.—*Chorus.*

WE'RE A BAND OF CHILDREN.

TUNE—"*Old Granite State.*"

1. To our homes we now are going,
   And God's love our hearts o'erflowing,
   And to whom all favors owing,
   To the blest Sabbath school.
     We're a band of children,
     We're a band of children,
     We're a band of children,
       Of the blest Sabbath school.

SOUND THE LOUD ANTHEM.

TUNE—"*Shout the glad tidings*," page 52.

1 " PRAISE to the grace which has triumphed so freely,
  Where sin had abounded and darkness had reigned;
  Praise to the word, which has spoken so fully
  Of blessings in store, which are yet to be gained.
    Sound the loud anthem o'er ocean and sea,
    The hand of Jehovah is stretched out to thee.

2. For Zebulon's sons yet " shall call to the mountain,"
  The people from far to the house of the Lord,
  To partake of that altar, and wash in that fountain
  Whose virtues their " going" shall herald abroad.
    Sound the loud anthem, &c.

3. The light of the promise already is dawning,
  For Zion is nursed by the ships of the sea;
  Her temples the sailor now gladly is thronging,
  Rejoiced from the bondage of sin to be free.
    Sound the loud anthem, &c.

4. On the shore, where his footsteps too often were taken
  In snares which the wicked had set for his feet,
  The Bethel now spreads for his welcome her beacon,
  And temples are rising his coming to greet.
    Sound the loud anthem, &c.

MRS. C. H. PUTNAM.

* Repeat 1st and 2d lines, 3d and 4th lines; also 5th and 6th lines.

THE SUNNY HOURS OF CHILDHOOD.

TUNE—"*Dewy Rose of Sharon*," S. S. BELL,
No. 2, p. 110.

1. THE sunny, sunny hours of childhood,
  How soon, how soon they pass away,
  Like flowers, like flowers in the wild wood,
    That once bloomed fresh and gay;
  But the perfume of the flowers,
    And the freshness of the heart,
  Live but a few brief hour,
    And then for aye depart.
  Cho. The sunny, sunny hours of childhood,
    How soon, how soon they pass away.

Like flowers, like flowers in the wild wood,
  That once bloomed fresh and gay.

2. The friends, the friends we saw around us,
  In boyhood's happy, happy days,
  The fairy, fairy links that bound us,
    No feeling now displays.
  For time hath changed for ever
    What youth can not retain,
  And we may know, ah! never
    Those sunny hours again.
    Chorus. The sunny, sunny hours, &c.

3. And yet, and yet again how fondly
  The scenes, the scenes of youth we trace;
  We bear, we hear a father's counsel,
    We see a tearful face.
  For a father's pious teachings,
    And a mother's holy tears,
  Have proved a lamp to guide us,
    These many, many years.
    Chorus. The sunny, sunny hours, &c.

J. E. CARPENTER.

TAKE MY HEART, O FATHER! TAKE IT.

TUNE—S. S. BELL, No. 1, p. 56

1. TAKE my heart, O Father! take it,
    Make and keep it all thine own;
  Let thy Spirit melt and break it,
    Turn to flesh this heart of stone.
  Heavenly Father, deign to mold it
    In obedience to thy will;
  And, as passing years, unfold it,
    Keep it meek and childlike still.

2. Father, make it pure and lowly,
    Peaceful, kind, and far from strife,
  Turning from the paths unholy,
    Of this vain and sinful life:
  May the blood of Jesus heal it,
    And its sins be all forgiven;
  Holy Spirit, take and seal it,
    Guide it in the path to heaven.

WE LOVE THE SABBATH DAY

Tune—Happy Land.

1. WE love the Sabbath day
    Best of the week ;
Here now we meet to pray,
    And Jesus seek.
O precious day of rest,
Day which God our Saviour blest,
Day which we love the best,
    Best of the week.

2. We love this sacred place—
    Dear Sabbath school ;
Here Jesus sheds his grace
    On every soul.
O may our hearts ascend
To our dearest Heavenly Friend,
Who loves us to the end,
    For evermore.

3. We love the precious truth
    God sent from Heaven ;
O may it guide our youth,
    While life is given.
Bright may it shine below,
Brighter as we farther go,
Till light eternal glow,
    Brightest in Heaven.

4. There filled with joy and peace
    We'll sweetly sing ;
Our songs shall never cease
    Praising our King.
While endless ages move
We shall feast upon his love,
And seraphs far above
    Join in our song.

FREDERICK COLLIER.

CHILDREN OF THE HEAVENLY KING.

Tune—Pleyel's Hymn.

1. CHILDREN of the heavenly King,
As ye journey, sweetly sing;
Sing your Saviour's worthy praise,
Glorious in his works and ways.

2. Ye are traveling home to God
In the way the fathers trod;
They are happy now, and ye
Soon their happiness shall see.

3. Sing, ye little flock, and blest :
You near Jesus' throne shall rest;
There your seats are now prepared,
There your kingdom and reward.

4. Lord, submissive make us go,
Gladly leaving all below ;
Only thou our Leader be,
And we still will follow thee.

OH, SUFFER THEM TO COME.

Tune—Shirland.

1. "OH, suffer them to come,"
Once the kind Saviour said,
And gently to his loving arms,
The little ones were led.

2. "Forbid them not," said He,
My ways are pleasant ways;
Children that fear and love my name,
Are happy all their days.

3. "Of such my kingdom is,"
The lowly and the meek;
Those who with sweet humility,
All my commandments keep.

4. We come, we come to Thee,
Dear Saviour, and would pray,
That from thy pleasant paths our feet
May never, never stray.

140

TEACHER, WATCH THE LITTLE FEET.

Words by G. W. Bungay.

Music by Lover. Arranged by Henry Tucker.

1. Teach-er, watch the lit - tle feet Walk-ing through the meadows fair,
2. Teach-er, watch the lit - tle hands, Bus - y, bus - y all the day,

Wand'ring thro' the crowd-ed street, Scarcely heard or noticed there.
Mak - ing forts with straws and sands, Pluck-ing ro - ses by the way.

DUET.

Nev - er count the la - bor lost, Nev - er heed the pains it cost,
Nev - er deem the la - bor lost, Nev - er heed the pains it cost,

CHORUS.

Lit - tle feet will go a - stray,
lit - tle hands here - af - ter may

Teacher, watch them while you may.
Na - tions and their his - t'ry sway.

3. Teacher, watch the little lips,
   Lisping sweet and pleasant words,
   Sometimes their soft utterance trips,
   Discord in the notes of birds.
   Never deem the labor lost,
   Never heed the pains it cost,
   Little lips "sometimes proclaim
   Blessings in a Saviour's name."

4. Teacher, watch the little heart,
   Pulsing here with hope and love,
   Truthful lessons here impart,
   Leading to our home above.
   Never deem the labor lost,
   Never heed the pains it cost,
   Little hearts hereafter may
   Control the children of to-day.

THE NOONDAY PRAYER-MEETING.
TUNE—"The Golden Rule."

1. FROM busy toil and heavy care
   We turn the weary mind,
   And in the place of noontide prayer
   Our sanctuary find.
   The midday hour, the noontide hour,
   It is the hour of prayer;
   Our souls receive renewing power,
   For Jesus meets us there.

2. The voice that stilled the stormy waves
   On distant Galilee,
   Speaks once again, and at the sound,
   Retires another sea.
   The midday hour, &c.

3. The restless waves of care and strife
   Obey the mighty voice;
   Peace broods the mighty waters o'er,
   And all our souls rejoice.
   The midday hour, &c.

4. These heaven-bright hours too soon are past;
   Grant, Lord, this greater boon:
   A place where worship never ends,
   Nor night succeeds to noon.
   The midday hour, &c.

IN THE GRAVE-YARD SOFTLY SLEEPING.

Words by G. W. Bungay. Music by C. S. Whitmore. Arranged by Henry Tucker.

CHORUS.

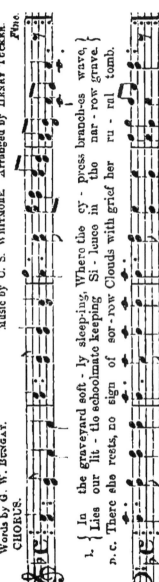

Fine.

1. { In the graveyard soft - ly sleeping, Where the cy - press branch-es wave, }
   { Lies our lit - tle schoolmate keeping Si - lence in the nar - row grave. }

D.C. There she rests, no sign of sor - row Clouds with grief her ru - ral tomb.

DUET.

D. C.

There she sleeps, and no to-mor-row Wakes her in that si - lent home;

2. There the daisies, and the roses,
   Pour their incense at her feet,
   On the spot where she reposes,
   Where the grass is green and sweet.
   There the wood-lark, sweetly singing,
   With her music charms the air:
   And the busy wild-bee winging,
   Hums a hymn for flowerets fair

3. But they can not wake our sister,
   On her bed within the tomb;
   Angels up in heaven missed her,
   So they came and took her home.
   'Took her where the wondrous glory
   Fills her happy soul with love,
   Where her heart can feel no sorrow
   In her blessed home above.

THE WINDS MAY BLOW. Infant Song.

Words by D.

Arranged by HENRY TUCKER.

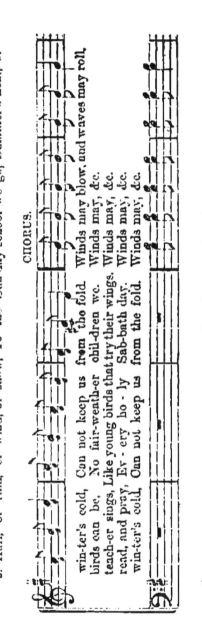

1. Hail, or rain, or wind, or snow, To the Sun-day school we go, Summer's heat, or
2. When the bell rings off we start, Quick of step, and light of heart, Hap-py, too, ns
3. How the minutes grow to hours, When these joy-ful hearts of ours, Beat the time the
4. In the bless-ed Sun-day school We are taught the golden rule, Here we sing, and
5. Hail, or rain, or wind, or snow, To the Sun-day school we go, Summer's heat, or

win-ter's cold, Can not keep us from the fold.
birds can be, No fair-weath-er obil-dren we.
teach-er sings, Like young birds that try their wings.
read, and pray, Ev - ery ho - ly Sab-bath day.
win-ter's cold, Can not keep us from the fold.

CHORUS.

Winds may blow, and waves may roll,
Winds may, &c.
Winds may, &c.
Winds may, &c.
Winds may, &c.

We will go to Sunday school, Winds may blow, waves may roll, We'll go to Sunday school.

144 Words by J. R. OSGOOD.

THERE IS A CLIME.

VENETIAN MELODY.
Arr. by HENRY TUCKER.

WHEN THE ROSY MORNING DAWNETH.

Words by Mrs. M. A. Kidder.

Scotch Melody. Arr. by A. Cull.

Allegretto. DUET.

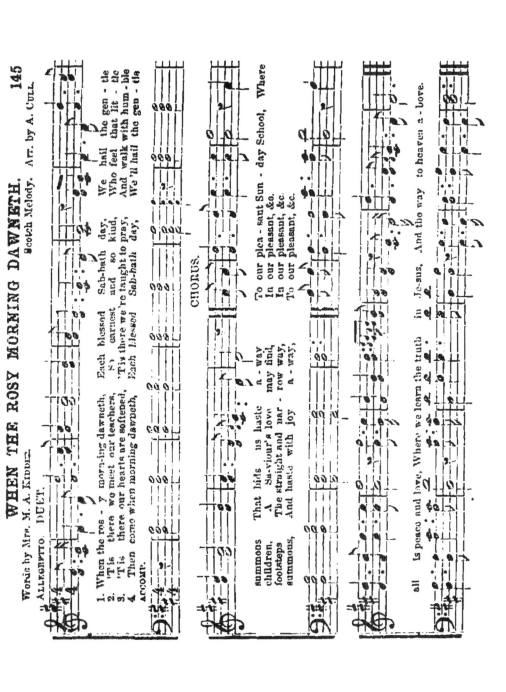

1. When the ros - y morning dawneth,   Each blessed Sab-bath day,   We hail the gen - tle
2. 'Tis there we meet our teachers,   So earnest and so kind,   Who feel that lit - tle
3. 'Tis there our hearts are softened,   'Tis there we're taught to pray,   And walk with hum - ble
4. Then come when morning dawneth,   Each blessed Sab-bath day,   We'll hail the gen - tle

accomp.

CHORUS.

summons   That bids us haste a - way   To our plea - sant Sun - day School, Where
children,   A Sa-viour's love may find,   In our pleasant, &c.
footsteps   The straight and nar - row way,   In our pleasant, &c.
summons,   And haste with joy a - way,   To our pleasant, &c.

all   Is peace and love, Where we learn the truth in Je-sus, And the way to heaven a - bove.

LAND OF OUR FATHERS. (CONCLUDED.)

join - ing, Sing we in har - mo - ny, Our na - tive land, Our na - tive land.

land. Our na - tive land. Our na - tive land, Our na - tive land

'Tho' other climes may brighter hopes fulfil,
Land of our birth! we ever love thee still :
Heaven shield our happy home from each hostile band,
Freedom and plenty ever crown our native land.

Full Chorus.—All then inviting, &c.

THERE WAS A PLACE IN CHILDHOOD.

SOLO, QUARTET, or CHORUS.

Arr. by JOHN GIBSON.

1. There was a place in childhood, That I re-member well; And there a voice of sweetest tone, Bright
2. When fai-ry tales were end-ed, "Good night," she softly said, And kiss'd, and laid me down to sleep, With-
3. In the sickness of my childhood, The pe-rils of my prime, The sorrows of my rip-er years, The

fai-ry tales did tell: And gentle words, and fond embrace, We're giv'n with joy to me, When I was in that
in my ti - ny bed : And holy words she taught me there, Methinks I yet can see Her angel eyes, as
cares of every time : When doubt or danger weigh'd me down, Then pleading all for me, It was a fer-vent

hap-py place, Up-on my mother's knee, My mother dear, My mother dear, My gen-tle, gen-tle mother.
close I knelt, Beside my mother's knee, My mother dear, &c.
prayer to heav'n, That bent my mother's knee, My mother dear, &c.

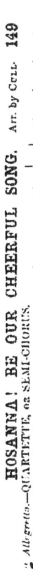

HOSANNA! BE OUR CHEERFUL SONG.

Arr. by Coll. 149

Allegretto.— QUARTETTE, or SEMI-CHORUS.

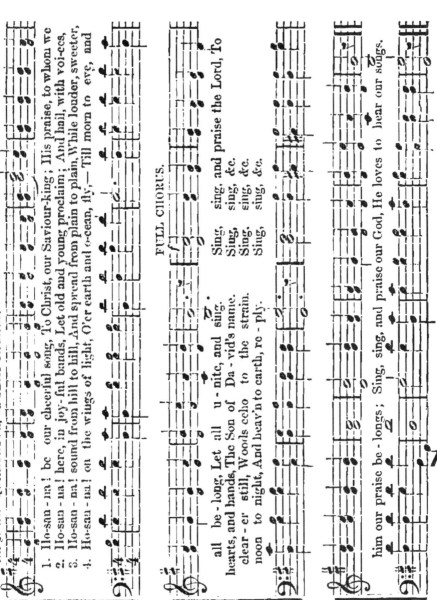

1. Ho-san - na! be our cheerful song, To Christ, our Saviour-king; His praise, to whom we
2. Ho-san - na! here, in joy-ful bands, Let old and young proclaim; And hail, with voi-ces,
3. Ho-san - na! sound from hill to hill, And spread from plain to plain, While louder, sweeter,
4. Ho-san - na! on the wings of light, O'er earth and o-cean, fly, — Till morn to eve, and

FULL CHORUS.

all be - long, Let all u - nite, and sing.   Sing,   sing, and praise the Lord, To
hearts, and hands, The Son of Da - vid's name.   Sing,   sing, &c.
clear - er still, Woods echo to the strain.   Sing,   sing, &c.
noon to night, And heav'n to earth, re - ply.   Sing,   sing, &c.

him our praise be - longs; Sing, sing, sing, and praise our God, He loves to hear our songs.

150   THOUGH I'M BUT A LITTLE MAIDEN;
or, GOD'S SO GOOD TO ME.*

Words by Mrs. M. A. Kidder.   Music arr. by A. Cull.

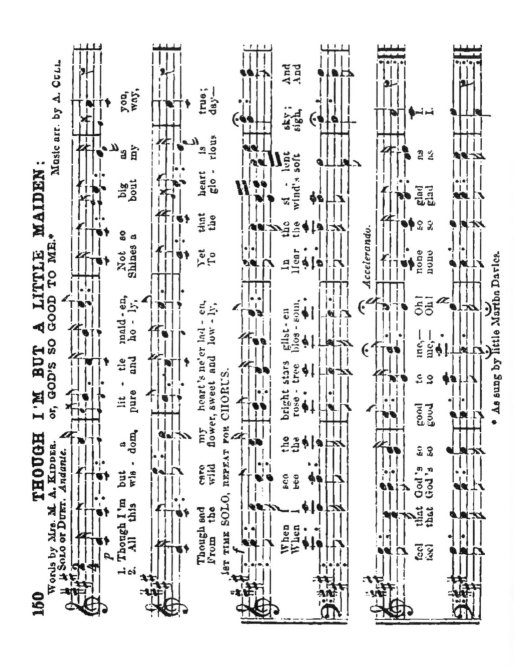

1. Though I'm but a lit-tle maid-en, Not so big as you,
2. All this wis-dom, pure and ho-ly, Shines a-bout my way,

Though and care my heart's ne'er lad-en, Yet faint the heart is true;
From the wild flower, sweet and low-ly, To the glo-rious day;—

1st time SOLO, repeat for CHORUS.

When I see the bright stars glist-en   In the si-lent sky;   And
When I too the rose-tree blos-som,   I hear the wind's soft sigh,   And

Accelerando.

feel that God's so good to me,—   Oh!   none so glad as I.
feel that God's so good to me,—   Oh!   none so glad as I.

* As sung by little Martha Davies.

3. I have watched the dark blue ocean,
   Restless in its pride,
And have felt my soul's devotion
   Leaping with the tide;
When I hear the brook's low music,
   Sweetly murmuring by,
And feel that God's so good to me—
   Oh! none so glad as I.

4. Loving friends are ever near me,
   Shielding me from wrong;
Gentle strangers press to hear me
   Sing my simple song;
When I know such care surrounds me,
   Love that can not die,
And feel that God's so good to me—
   Oh! none so glad as I.

TEMPERANCE CALL

Tune—page 123.

1. Children all, both great and small,
   Answer to the temp'rance call;
Mary, Marg'ret, Jane, and Sue,
Charlotte, Ann, and Fanny too,
Chorus—Cheerily, heartily, come along,
Sign our pledge, and sing our song.

2. No strong drink shall pass our lips,
He's in danger who but sips.
Come, then, children, one and all,
Answer to the temp'rance call.
   Chor. Cheerily, &c.

3. Where's the boy that would not shrink
From the bondage of strong drink?
Come, then, Joseph, Charles, and Tom,
Henry, Samuel, James, and John.
   Chor. Cheerily, &c.

4. Who have misery, want and wo?
And who to the bottle go?
We resolve their road to shun,
And in temp'rance paths to run.
   Chor. Cheerfully, &c.

5. Good cold water does for us;
Costs no money, makes none worse,
Gives no bruises, steals no brains;
Breeds no quarrels, woes, nor pains.
   Chor. Readily, &c.

6. Who would life and health prolong?
Who'd be happy, wise, and strong?
Let alone the drunkard's bane,
Half-way pledges are in vain.
   Chor. Cheerfully, joyfully, you and yon.
   Sign the pledge, and keep it too.

LITTLE SCHOOLMATES, CAN YOU TELL

Tune—S. Bell, No. 1, p. 51.

FIRST CLASS.

1. Little schoolmates, can you tell
Who has kept us safe and well
Through the watches of the night,
Brought us safe to see the light?

SECOND CLASS.

2. Yes; it is our God doth keep
Little children while they sleep;
He has kept us safe from harm,
Sheltered by his powerful arm.

FIRST CLASS.

3. Can you tell who gives us food,
Clothes, and home, and parents good,
Schoolmates dear, and teachers kind,
Useful books, and active mind?

SECOND CLASS.

4. Yes; our heavenly Father's care
Gives us all we eat and wear;
All our books, and all our friends,
God, in kindness, to us sends.

CHORUS.

5. Oh, then, let us thankful be,
For his mercies large and free;
Every morning let us raise
Our young voices in his praise.

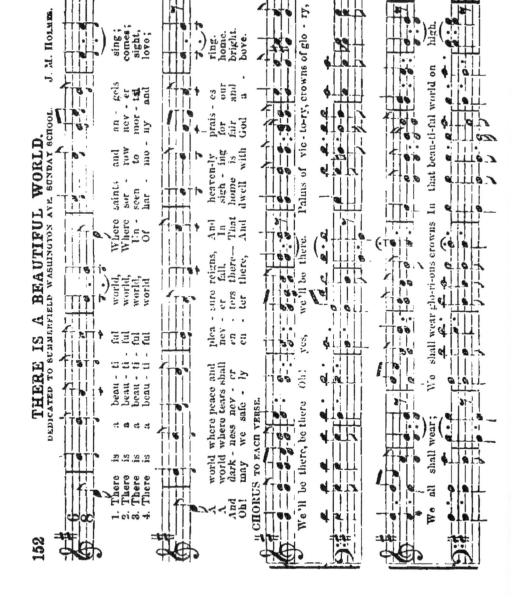

THERE IS A BEAUTIFUL WORLD.

DEDICATED TO SUMMERFIELD WASHINGTON AVE. SUNDAY SCHOOL.

J. M. HOLME.

152

SPARKLING AND BRIGHT.

Words by Mrs. S. E. Dana.　　Music arranged by H. Waters.

1. Spark - ling and bright in its li - quid light, Is the wa - ter in our glass - es;
'T will give you health, 't will give you wealth, Ye lads and ro - sy lass - - es.

CHORUS.

Oh, then re - sign, your ru - by wine, Each smil - ing son and daugh - ter,

There's nothing so good for the youth-ful blood, Or sweet as the sparkling wa - ter.

2. Better than gold is the water cold,
　　From the crystal fountain flowing;
　A calm delight, both day and night,
　　To happy homes bestowing.
　　　Chorus.—Oh, then resign, &c.

3. Sorrow has fled from the heart that bled—
　　Of the weeping wife and mother,
　　They'd given up the poisoned cup,
　　Son, husband, daughter, brother.
　　　Chorus.—Oh, then resign, &c.

154   A LITTLE WORD IN KINDNESS SAID.

Arranged by H. Waites.

2. A word, a look, has crushed to earth
Full many a budding flower,
:|: Which, had a smile but owned its birth,
Would bless life's darkest hour. :|

3. Then deem it not an idle thing,
A pleasant word to speak :
:|: The face you wear, the thoughts you bring,
A heart may heal or break :|:

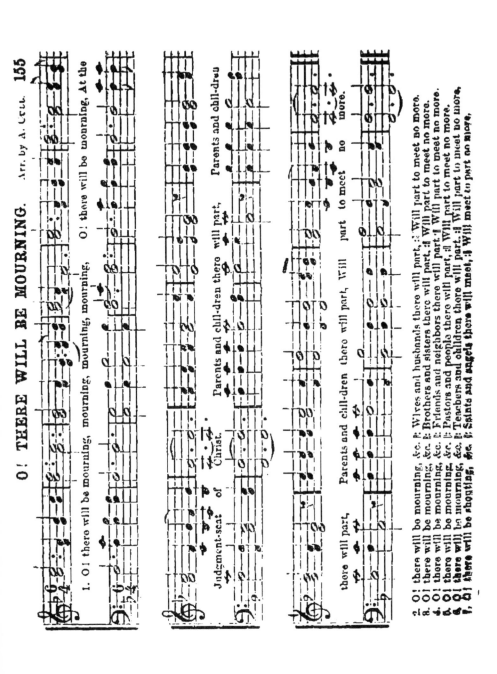

O! THERE WILL BE MOURNING.

Arr. by A. Clell. 155

1. O! there will be mourning, mourning, mourning, mourning, O! there will be mourning, At the

Judgment-seat of Christ.

Parents and chil-dren there will part, Parents and chil-dren

there will part, Parents and chil-dren there will part, Will part to meet no more.

Will part to meet no more.

2. O! there will be mourning, &c. ‖: Wives and husbands there will part, :‖ Will part to meet no more.
3. O! there will be mourning, &c. ‖: Brothers and sisters there will part, :‖ Will part to meet no more.
4. O! there will be mourning, &c. ‖: Friends and neighbors there will part, ‖ Will part to meet no more.
5. O! there will be mourning, &c. ‖: Pastors and people there will part, ‖ Will part to meet no more.
6. O! there will be mourning, &c. ‖: Teachers and children there will part, :‖ Will part to meet no more,
7. O! there will be shouting, &c. ‖: Saints and angels there will meet, :‖ Will meet to part no more,

MY BROTHER, I WISH YOU WELL!

Arr. by H. Waters.

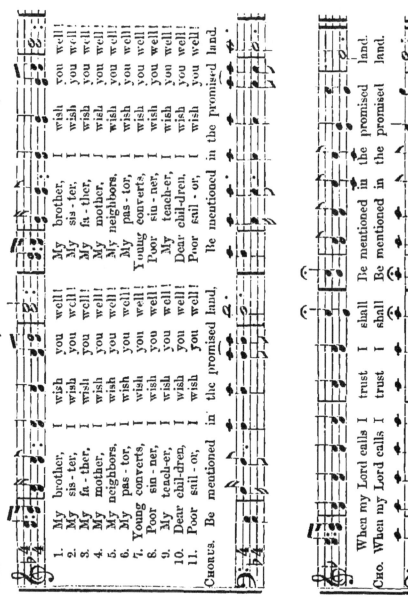

1. My brother,   I wish you well!   My brother,   I wish you well!
2. My sis-ter,   I wish you well!   My sis-ter,   I wish you well!
3. My fa-ther,   I wish you well!   My fa-ther,   I wish you well!
4. My mother,   I wish you well!   My mother,   I wish you well!
5. My neighbors,   I wish you well!   My neighbors,   I wish you well!
6. My pas-tor,   I wish you well!   My pas-tor,   I wish you well!
7. Young converts,   I wish you well!   Young converts,   I wish you well!
8. Poor sin-ner,   I wish you well!   Poor sin-ner,   I wish you well!
9. My teach-er,   I wish you well!   My teach-er,   I wish you well!
10. Dear chil-dren,   I wish you well!   Dear chil-dren,   I wish you well!
11. Poor sail-or,   I wish you well!   Poor sail-or,   I wish you well!

CHORUS. Be mentioned in the promised land,   Be mentioned in the promised land.

When my Lord calls I trust I shall   Be mentioned in the promised land.

Cho. When my Lord calls I trust I shall   Be mentioned in the promised land.

THERE ARE ANGELS HOVERING ROUND.

Arr. by A. C'ull.

165.

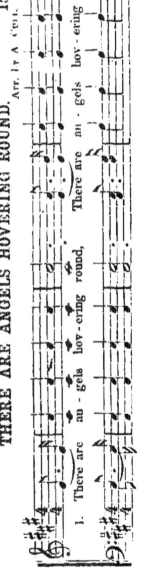

1. There are an - gels hov - ering round,   There are an - gels hov - ering

round. There are an - - gels, an   -   gels, an   - - gels hov - - ering round.

2. To carry the tidings home
   To the New Jerusalem.

3. Poor sinners are coming home,
   And Jesus bids them come.

4. Let him that thirsteth come,
   And drink while yet there's room.

5. He's waiting for you now,
   Before his throne to bow.

6. Repent, on him believe,
   And his rich grace receive.

7. We are on our journey home,
   Where Christ our Lord has gone.

8. Our friends who have gone before,
   Stand waiting on the shore—

9. Inviting us, in love,
   To their bright home above.

10. Our sorrows being o'er,
    We shall meet to part no more.

11. We shall live for evermore
    On Canaan's happy shore.

ABOUT THIS HEAVENLY UNION.

Arranged by H. W.

1. Attend, ye saints, and hear me tell The wonders of Im-man-u-el, Who saved me from a burning hell, And brought my soul with him to dwell, And feel this blessed u - nion.

2. When Jesus saw me from on high,
Beheld my soul in ruin lie,
He looked on me with pitying eye,
And said to me as he passed by,
"With God you have no union."

3. Then I began to weep and cry,
And looked this way and that, to fly,
It grieved me so that I must die;
I strove salvation for to buy:
But still I had no union.

4. But when I hated all my sin,
My dear Redeemer took me in,
And with his blood he washed me clean,
And oh! what seasons I have seen
Since first I felt this union.

5. I praised the Lord both night and day,
And went from house to house to pray,
And when I met one on the way,
I always had something to say
About this heavenly union.

THE PRECIOUS SABBATH SCHOOL.

Composed by Rev. J. M. Thomas, Pitsburg, Pa.

1. Love - ly is the dawn O' each ris- ing day: Lovell - est the morn Of the Sabbath day:
2. All the week we spend Full of youth and bliss: Ev- ery changing scene Brings its happi - ness;

Yet our joys would not be full Had we not the Sabbath school, Had we not the Sabbath school.
Yet no joys are half as full As we meet at Sabbath school As we meet at Sabbath school.

3. Why do children stay
   From this source of joy?
   What we learn to-day
   Time cannot destroy;
   And we wish the seats were full
   At this precious Sabbath school.

4. Teachers, you are kind
   Thus to point the road,
   Leading me from sin
   To our Father, God;
   And our joys are ever full
   When we are at Sabbath school.

JESUS ON THE CROSS.

Words by the author of "*I want to be an angel.*" Music by Mr. DAVID WARDEN

"And, sitting down, they watched Him there." Matt. xxvii. 36; Zech. xii. 10; Lam. i. 12; Psalm xxii. 27; John xii. 32.

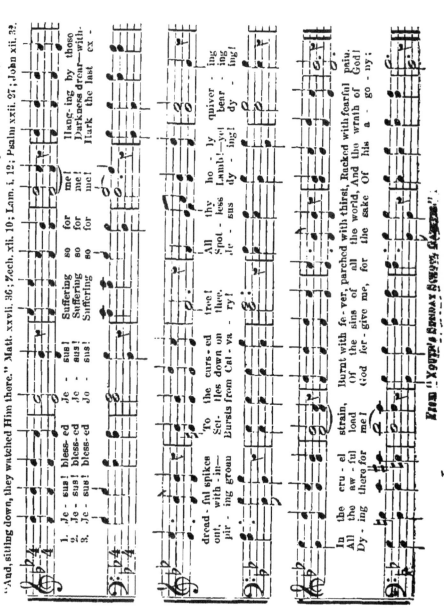

WANDERING STRANGER.

Arr. by A. Cull.

1. "Say, which-er, wandering stranger, Ah! whither dost thou roam? O'er this wide world a-
2. "But want and woe have driv-en The ro - ses from thy cheek; And garments rent and
3. "Come, then, be-nign in-quir - er, And join me on my way; I'm journeying to a

ran - ger, Hast thou no friend, no home?" "Yes, I've a Friend who nev - er Is
riv - en, Thy pov - er - ty he - speak." "I've food with which the an - gels Would
coun - try Where beams an end - less day; "Where saints and an - gels, full - ing Be -

ab - sent from my side; And I've a home wher-ev - er In peace I shall a - bide.
all de - light-ed be; And robes of dazzling brightness Are now a - wait-ing me.
fore the great, white throne, To you, to me are call - ing, Haste, pilgrim, hast-en home."

AWAY TO SABBATH SCHOOL.

Arr. by A. Coll.

1. { The morning sun is bright and clear; Away to Sabbath school; }
   { Let each one in his class appear; Away to Sabbath school; } 'Tis there we learn his holy word, And
2. { In season let us all be there; Away to Sabbath school; }
   { That we may join the opening prayer; Away to Sabbath school; } There we can raise our hearts to heaven, And

find the road that leads to God: A - way, a - way, a - way, a - way, A - way to Sabbath school.
praise the Lord for blessings given: A - way, a - way, &c.

SCHOLARS.

3. When each at night shall go to prayer,
   We'll ask our God above
   To extend o'er teachers his kind care,
   And crown them with his love.
   And when on earth our time is sped,
   And we are numbered with the dead,

TEACHERS AND SCHOLARS.

   If faithful, we shall meet above—
   We all shall meet above.

4. Let us remember, while at prayer,
   When at the Sabbath school,
   Our teachers' kindness, and their care
   Towards our Sabbath school.
   We'll be submissive, good, and kind,
   And every rule and order mind
   When we're at school, at Sabbath school
   When we're at Sabbath school

'TIS WELL.

Words and Music by Rev. ROBERT LOWRY.

164.

A HOME BEYOND THE TIDE.

Wm. B. Bradbury. From "Oriola," by permission

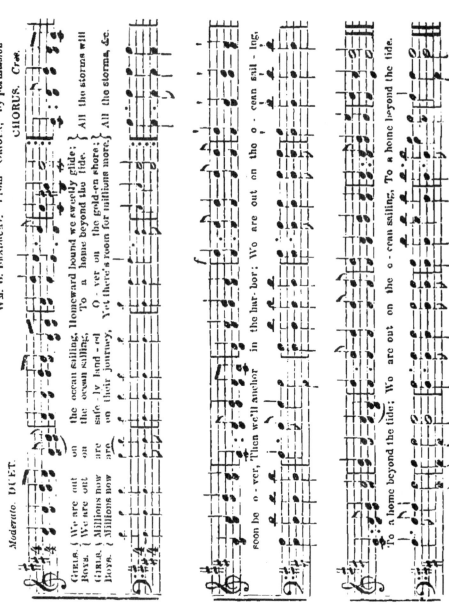

3. Come on board, O! "ship" for glory,
   Be in haste—make up your mind!
   For our vessel's weighing anchor,
   You will soon be left behind!
   Cho.—All the storms, &c.

4. You have kindred over yonder,
   On that bright and happy shore,
   By-and-by we'll swell the number,
   When the toils of life are o'er.
   Cho.—All the storms, &c.

5. Spread your sails, while heavenly breezes
   Gently waft our vessel on ;
   All on board are sweetly singing—
   Free salvation is the song.
   Cho.—All the storms, &c.

6. When we all are safely anchored,
   We will shout—our trials o'er!
   We will walk about the city,
   And we'll sing for evermore.
   Cho.—All the storms, &c.

DEAR JESUS, LET THY PITYING EYE.

"Suffer little children to come unto me,"

TUNE—*Balerma.*

1. Dear Jesus, let thy pitying eye
   Look kindly down on me:
   A sinful, weak, and helpless child,
   I come thy child to be.

2. O blessed Saviour, take my heart,
   This sinful heart of mine,
   And wash it clean in every part;
   Make me a child of thine.

3. My sins, though great, thou canst forgive,
   For you hast died for me;
   Amazing love! Help me, O God,
   Thine own dear child to be.

4. For thou hast said, "Forbid them not:
   Let children come to me;"
   I hear thy voice, and now, dear Lord,
   I come thy child to be.   LEILA IKE

WE MEET AGAIN.

TUNE—*"The morning light is breaking."*

1. We meet again in gladness,
   And thankful voices raise;
   To God, our heavenly Father,
   We'll tune our grateful praise :
   'Tis his kind hand that kept us
   Through all the changing year ;
   His love it is that brings us
   Again to worship here.

2. We'll thank him for the Sabbath,
   This day of holy rest;
   And for the blessed Bible,
   The book that we love best ;
   For Sabbath-schools and teachers,
   To us so kindly given,
   To guide us in the pathway
   That leads to joy in heaven.

3. We'll thank him for our country,
   The land our fathers trod ;
   For liberty of conscience,
   And right to worship God.
   O Lord! our heavenly Father,
   Accept the praise we bring,
   And tune our hearts and voices
   Thy glorious name to sing.

4. Soon may thy gracious sceptre
   Extend to every land,
   And all as willing subjects
   Submit to thy command.
   Send forth the gospel tidings,
   And hasten on the day
   When every isle and nation
   Shall own Messiah's sway.

166

SHOUT THE TIDINGS.

Rev. R. Lowry.

5. Shout the tidings of salvation,
   Till the world shall hear the call,
   And with joyous acclamation
   Crown the Saviour Lord of all. *Chorus.*

REST WITH JESUS.

Words by Rev. Sarah Dyer.

Music arranged by Horace Waters.

Andantino. DUET or SEMI-CHORUS.

1st time.

1. { Faith, hope, love, are a - wa - king joy, joy in the sad breast,
Cares, pains, sins all for - sa - king,

2. { Come, come, la - den and wea - ry, Sick, sore, sad - ly op - prest,
Lone, lost tread-ing life drea - ry,

FULL CHORUS.

2d time.

Sweetly in Je - sus we rest.
Come to the Saviour and rest.

Aye, all, full, free, Sweetly in Je - sus find rest.
Come, now, one, all, Come un-to Je - sus and rest.

3. Old, young, all are invited;
Rich, poor, come and be blest;
Trust, love, serve, and united,
Jesus will give thee his rest
Cho.—Aye, full, free, sweet,
Jesus will give thee his rest

4. Now, now, while yet 'tis early,
Lord, Lord, hear our request,
Guide us up to gates pearly,
Bid us there enter and rest.
Cho.—There, saved, robed, crowned,
Ever with Jesus to rest.

168

WAVE WILLOWS, MURMUR WATERS.

Words and Music by H. S. Thompson.   Arr. by H. Waters.

Moderato. SOLO or DUET.

1. Down where the wav-ing wil-lows, 'Neath the sun-beams smile:
Pure as the for-est lil-y, Nev-er thought of guile

2. Sweet, came the hallowed chim-ing Of the Sab-bath bell,
On a bed of pain and an-guish, Lay dear An-nie Lisle;

Shadowed o'er the murm'ring wa-ters, Dwelt sweet An-nie Lisle;
Had its home with-in the bo-som Of sweet An-nie Lisle
Borne on the morn-ing breez-es Down the wood-y dell.
Chang-ed were the love-ly features, Gone the hap-py smile.

CHORUS.

Wave willows, murmur waters, Golden sunbeams smile; Earthly music cannot waken Lovely Annie Lisle.

REPEAT CHORUS *pp*

3. Toll bells of Sabbath morning,
I shall never more
Hear your sweet and holy music,
On this earthly shore.
Forms clad in heav'nly beauty
Look on me and smile:
Waiting for the longing spirit
Of your Annie Lisle. *Cho.*

Raise me in your arms, dear Mother,
Let me once more look
On the green and waving willows,
And the flowing brook;
Hark, those strains of angel music
From the choirs above;
Dearest Mother, I am going,
Truly, "God is love." *Cho.*

By permission of OLIVER DITSON & Co., Boston.

JESUS ONCE CAME.

Words by Rev. Sidney Dyer.

Music arr. by A Coll.

SOLO or DUET.

1. { When Jesus once came to Jerusalem's gate, The crowds rushed along like the floods from the fountain; }
   { With a tribute of palms on his triumph they wait, And ho-sannas re - echo round Olivet's mountain. }

Had their lips ceased to cry as the Saviour passed by, The rocks in their rapture would herald him nigh:

CHORUS.

O let our glad voices their chief honors bring, Still shouting hos-annas to Je - sus our King!

2. He comes to the weary with rest for the soul,
   To bind up the heart that affliction has broken,
   At his life-giving presence the sin-sick are whole,
   And the poor are enriched by some priceless love token.
   Every bosom is stirred as they hear the blest word,
   That Jesus has come in the name of the Lord ;
   CHORUS.
   And shouting with gladness, their chief honors bring,
   Hosannas and blessings to Jesus their King!

3. O Saviour, we long for thy coming again,
   That Zion may greet thee with new acclamations ;
   And the song of redemption by Him that was slain,
   Be thy tribute of praise from the lips of all nations.
   O that thrice blessed day when the ransomed shall say,
   " Behold the King cometh! he passes this way!"
   CHORUS.
   And joining their voices, shall evermore sing,
   Hosannas and blessings to Jesus our King!

BEHOLD A HOST.

Words by S. Dinn
Music arr. by A. Corll

170 Marciale e con fuoco
SEMI-CHORUS.

1. Behold a host with rapt e - mo - tion, Before the great white throne are bow'd; Their hymns swell
2. Arrayed in shin-ing robes of glo - ry, All number-less those throngs up-pear; An El-der,
3. Ah, blessed land! where eyes are tear-less, All pain is past, and sin unknown: Where every

up of deep de - vo - tion, Like ma - ny wa - ters break-ing loud, Like ma - ny
versed in sa - cred sto - ry, Asks, "whence are these thus thronging here?" Asks, "whence are
joy is pure and peer-less, And rap-ture breathes in ev - ery tone. And rap-ture

DUET.

wa - ters break-ing loud; "All wor-thy is the Lamb, once low - ly, To be ex -
these thus throng-ing here?" Ah, these come up from tri - bu - la - tion, Their robes have
breathes in ev - ery tone. There Je - sus reigns, who once was low - ly, And soon be

BEHOLD A HOST. (CONCLUDED.)

altered evermore,
The Lord our God, whom we adore,
As ever crying, holy,

washed from every stain,
In his rich blood, who once was slain,
For every kindred, tongue, and

fore him we shall stand,
Among that host, with harp in hand,
With angels crying, holy,

FULL CHORUS.

holy!   A-men!   A-men we sing!   To us   the hope is given:—Press
nation!   A-men!   A-men we sing!   That precious blood was given:—Press
holy!   A-men!   A-men we sing!   That such a hope was given:—Press

press on!   the conflict o'er,   that host in heaven!   We'll join
on!   that fountain's near,   and enter heaven!   We'll wash,
on!   we're going home,   the host of heaven!   To join

press on!
on!
on!

172

SABBATH SCHOOL BELLS, CHIME ON.

Words by AUSTRALIE. Music by Rev. R. LOWRY.

SABBATH SCHOOL BELLS, CHIME ON. (Concluded.)

Chime on, chime on,... chime on, chime on, chime on, sweet bells, chime on, sweet bells, chime

Chime on,.......... chime on,..........

on, sweet bells, chime on, sweet bells, chime on, sweet bells, chime on, sweet bells, chime on.

2.

We leave our books and play,
To read that "Book Divine;"
There we are taught the way
To joys that ne'er decline;
The music of those Sabbath bells,
How sweetly on the ear it swells!

Cho.—Chime on, loved bells, your welcome ring,
Shall tune our hearts God's praise to sing.

3.

We leave our earthly home,
To seek that blest abode,
Where loved companions come
To lift their hearts to God;
List to the joyous sound that tells
The music of those Sabbath bells;

Cho.—Chime on, sweet bells, long may your ring
Inspire our hearts God's praise to sing.

DYING IS BLISS. (CONCLUDED.)

ff FULL CHORUS.

bears to his love! HOME, HEAVEN, and Jesus when I can see, Dy-ing is bliss, for it
dy-ing we crave. HOME, HEAVEN, &c.

bears me to thee, Dy-ing is bliss, for it bears me to thee!

LITTLE EFFORTS.

1. A LITTLE child I am, indeed,
   And little do I know;
   Much help and care I yet shall need,
   That I may wiser grow,
   If I would ever hope to do
   Things great and good, and useful too.

2. But even now I ought to try
   To do what good I may;
   God never meant that such as I
   Should only live to play,
   And talk, and laugh, and eat, and drink,
   And sleep, and wake, and never think

3. One gentle word that I may speak,
   Or one kind, loving deed,
   May, though a trifle, poor and weak,
   Prove like a tiny seed;
   And who can tell what good may spring
   From such a very little thing?

4. Then let me try, each day and hour,
   To act upon this plan:
   What little good is in my power,
   To do it while I can.
   If to be useful thus I try,
   I may be better by and by.

176   OUR HEARTS ARE YOUNG AND JOYOUS.*

Words by Mrs. E. I. Knowles.

Music by A. J. Vail.

1. Our hearts are young and joy-ous, 'Tis spring-time with us now; The dew of life's bright
2. The smil-ing sun of sum-mer, The bloom-ing buds and flowers, The gentle rain de-

morn - ing is fresh up - on each brow. The world to us seems pleas - ant, We
scend - ing in soft, re - freshing showers; The love of those who love us

love its joys to share; God, in his ten - der kind - ness, Hath
kind - ness of our friends, All those good gifts re - mind us, God's

* From "Sunday School Advocate."

made it ver - y fair, God, in his ten - der kind - ness, Hath made it very fair.
goodness nev - er ends, All these good gifts remind us God's goodness never ends.

3. O can we e'er forget him
   Who is so good and kind?
   No; rather would we love him
   With all our heart and mind.
   But we can never love him
   Until our hearts are clean;
   The precious blood of Jesus
   Must wash them first from sin.

4. We know he died to save us,
   We know he lives above;
   We know that every moment
   He watches us with love.
   We know that he has called us
   To early come to him;
   We know that he is willing
   The youngest to redeem.

5. We know the harps of heaven
   Would sound a gladder strain;
   "There's joy among the angels"
   When one repents of sin.
   O help us, then, dear Saviour,
   To give our hearts to thee;
   Let us, in youth's glad morning,
   Thy loved disciples be!

6. And when upon our foreheads
   The silver locks shall fall;
   Or early comes the shadow,
   Which comes alike to all,

Still safe upon thy bosom
Our spirits shall recline,
And 'mid the joys of heaven
We shall be ever thine!

SISTER, THOU WAST MILD AND LOVELY.

TUNE—"*Mount Vernon.*"

1. SISTER, thou wast mild and lovely,
   Gentle as the summer breeze,
   Pleasant as the air of evening
   When it floats among the trees.

2. Peaceful be thy silent slumber,
   Peaceful in the grave so low;
   Thou no more wilt join our number,
   Thou no more our songs shalt know.

3. Dearest sister, thou hast left us,
   Here thy loss we deeply feel;
   But 'tis God that hath bereft us,
   He can all our sorrows heal.

4. Yet again we hope to meet thee,
   When the day of life is fled,
   Then in heaven, with joy to greet thee,
   Where no farewell tear is shed.

178

THE HEAVENLY LAND.

Words by Mrs. M. A. Kiddle

Music by Glover. Arr. by A. Cecil.

1st Voice, Soprano Solo.

1. Heaven - ly land! beau - ti - ful land! How I long on thy peaceful shore to stand, Where the
2. Heaven - ly land! beau - ti - ful land! Oh, when shall I walk o'er the gold - en sands Of thy
3. Heaven - ly land! beau - ti - ful land! Our cl - ty, sweet Zion, se - cure - ly stands;

crys - tal ri - ver flows pure and bright, And the Pas - chal Lamb is the glorious light, And the
wel - come shores to the pearl - y gates, Where a white-robed throng shall my soul a - walt, Where a
Bride of the Saviour, so fair to see, None but the ho - ly can dwell with thee.

2d Solo Voice, Alto.

Pas - chal Lamb is the glo-rious light, 'Tis then I'll meet with the friends I know, Tho
white-robed throng shall my soul a - walt. Where fade - less flow'rs in their beauty bloom, In the
None but the ho - ly can dwell with thee. Grant me, Lord, but a hum-ble seat, But a

loved who have gone from this world be-low, And we'll be a hap-py end lov - ing band, When we
beau-ti - ful host, he-yond the tomb, There we'll be a hap-py and lov - ing band, When, &c.
low - ly place at the Saviour's feet, Where I may join with the en - gel band, When, &c

rall.

meet on the shore of the hea-ven-ly land, When we meet on the shore of the hea-ven-ly land

THE HEAVENLY LAND. (CONCLUDED.)

JESUS! JESUS! PRECIOUS SAVIOUR!

Words and Music by C. HATCH SMITH, A. M.

Con Spirito.

1st time. | 2d time. FINE.

1. { Je - sus! Je - sus! precious Saviour! Prophet! Priest, and King!
Wonder! wonder! God and mor-till } (omit.) Un-to thee we sing.

Chorus. Je - sus! Je - sus! precious Saviour! &c.

D. C. AL FINE.

Inst.

Proudly! proudly! may thy banner Float o'er all the world!
May! oh! may the heavenly standard, (omit.) } Never, nev - er, once be furled.

2. Wisely! wisely! taught by Jesus—
Gird we on the sword;
Bravely! bravely! where He leads us—
Wield it for our Lord!
Nobly! nobly! strive for Jesus
Until life is done!
Eager! eager! precious Saviour!
For thy glorious crown! Chorus.

3. Closely! closely! Holy Spirit!
Link with Heav'n each soul!
Surely! surely! break the earth-ties—
Take from sin's control!
Jesus! Jesus! be Thou near us,
Give to each thy grace;
Let us—let us with the ransomed
See thy glorious face. Chorus.

BROTHER, THOU ART GONE TO REST.*

From PSALTERY. By permission.

AFFETTUOSO.

2. Brother, thou art gone to rest;
   Thine is an earthly tomb;
   But Jesus summon'd thee away,
   Thy Saviour call'd thee home.

3. Brother, thou art gone to rest;
   Thy toils and cares are o'er;
   And sorrow, pain, and suff'ring, now
   Shall ne'er distress thee more.

4. Brother, thou art gone to rest;
   Thy sins are all forgiv'n;
   And saints in light have welcom'd thee,
   To share the joys of heav'n.

5. Brother, thou art gone to rest;
   And this shall be our pray'r;
   That, when we reach our journey's end,
   Thy glory we may share.

* Sister, Teacher, or Schoolmate, can be used in place of Brother.

182

THE LORD IS MY SHEPHERD.

Arr. by A. Cull.

1. The Lord is my Shepherd, how hap-py am I! How tender and watchful my wants to sup-ply!
2. The Lord is my Shepherd, then must I o - bey His gracious commandment, and walk in his way —
3. The Lord is my Shepherd, how hap-py am I! I'm blest while I live, and I'm blest when I die,
4. "The Lord is my Shepherd," I'll sing with delight, Till called to a - dore him in re-gions of light;

He dai-ly pro-vides me with raiment and food, Whate'er he de-signs me is meant for my good,
His fear he will teach me, my heart he 'll renew, And tho' I'm so sin-ful, My sins he'll sub-due.
In death's gloomy val-ley no e - vil I'll dread, "For I will be with thee," my Shepherd has said.
Then praise him, with an-gels, to bright harps of gold, And ev - er and ev - er his glo-ry be - hold.

THE MORNING OF REST.

1.

How sweet is the Sabbath, the morning of rest!
The day of the week which I surely love best;
The morning my Saviour arose from the tomb,
And took from the grave all its terror and gloom

2.

O let me be thoughtful and prayerful to-day,
And not spend a minute in trifling or play;
Remembering these seasons were graciously given
To teach me to seek, and prepare me for heaven.

SABBATH SCHOOL AND REVIVAL BOOKS PUBLISHED BY THIS HOUSE.

THE ANNIVERSARY AND SUNDAY SCHOOL MUSIC BOOK, NUMBER ONE, contains 32 tunes and hymns. Price 3 cents each, $2 per hundred, 1 cent each postage.

   NUMBER TWO, contains 36 tunes and hymns.   Price 3 cents, $2 per hundred.

   NUMBER THREE, contains 80 tunes and hymns.   Price 4 cents, $3 per hundred.

   NUMBER FOUR, contains 36 tunes and hymns.   Price 3 cents, $2 per hundred.

   NUMBER FIVE, contains 50 tunes and hymns.   Price 5 cents, $3 per hundred.

   NUMBER SIX, contains 64 pages.   Price 8 cents, $5 per hundred.

   NUMBER SEVEN, contains 70 pages.   Price 8 cents, $5 per hundred.

THE ANNIVERSARY AND SUNDAY SCHOOL MUSIC BOOK, combining NUMBERS ONE and TWO, with several additional pieces, contains 73 tunes and hymns.   Price 8 cents, $5 per hundred.

REVIVAL MUSIC BOOK, combining NUMBERS ONE and TWO, with twenty additional pieces, contains 73 tunes and hymns.   Price 8 cents, $5 per hundred.

SABBATH SCHOOL BELL, NUMBER ONE, contains nearly 200 tunes and hymns, and is one of the best collections ever issued.   Price 12 cents, $10 per hundred, postage 2 cents.   Bound 20 cents, $15 per hundred, postage 3 cents.   Elegantly bound in cloth, embossed gilt, 25 cents, $20 per hundred.   Ditto, in cloth and Turkey morocco, embossed gilt, gilt edge, etc., prices 40 cents to $1.

Nearly 1,000,000 of these books have been issued the past three years, and the demand is increasing.

SABBATH SCHOOL BELL, NUMBER TWO, just issued, contains some 40 more pages than BELL, NUMBER ONE. The words and music are all different, and as good, if not better, than BELL, NUMBER ONE.   Price, paper covers, 15 cents, $12 per hundred, postage 3 cents.   Bound, 25 cents, $18 per hundred, postage 6 cents.   Elegantly bound, embossed gilt, 30 cents, $25 per hundred, postage 6 cents.   Ditto, in cloth and Turkey morocco, embossed gilt, gilt edge, etc., prices from 45 cents to $1.   BELLS, NUMBERS ONE and TWO, bound, 40 cents, $30 per hundred; elegantly bound, embossed gilt, 50 cents, $40 per hundred, postage 9 cents.

SHEET MUSIC, WITH PIANO ACCOMPANIMENT,

PUBLISHED BY

HORACE WATERS, Agt., No. 333 BROADWAY, NEW YORK.

SACRED SONGS, DUETS, TRIOS, QUARTETTS AND CHORUSSES.

Music of Angels. Duet................ .25
Kind Words can Never Die. Duet and Chorus .25
Happy Christmas Morn. Duet and Chorus ...25
I ought to Love my Mother. Duet........... .25
Beautiful Zion. Quartette................ .25
The Angels told me so. Duet and Chorus...... .25
Though I'm but a Little Maiden; or, God's so
Good to me. Song, or Duet and Chorus..... .25
When Light comes o'er the Plain. Duet........ .25
Cantata—Announcement of the Saviour's Birth,
and Singing of the Gospel by Angels. Solos,
Trio and Chorus................. .40
My Mother, dear, I Fondly Love. Song. ...... .25
Has Sorrow thy Bright Morn Clouded. Duet... .25
Like the Last Leaf of Autumn. Song or Duet.. .25
Christmas Bells. Solo, Duet and Quartette..... .30
Thoughts of God. Song................ .25
I'm with thee still. Song............ .25
Don't you hear the Angels coming. Solo, Duet
and Chorus................. .25
Behold a Host with rapt emotion. Du. and Qh..25
There is a Beautiful World. Solo and Chorus.. .25
There was a place in Childhood. Song........ .25
Then the Rosy Morning Dawneth. Duet and
Chorus................. .25
Heaven Bless the School. Solo, Duet and Cho. .25
The Dewy Rose of Sharon Song and Chorus .. .25

SECULAR SONGS.

Jonny's so Bashful................. .25
Willie Gray; or, Answer to Kitty Clyde. Song .25
Maidens' Wish. Song................ .25
Wilds of the West. Song............ .25
'Tis hard to give the Hand where the Heart can
never be. Song................ .25
Family Meeting. Song and Chorus........ .25
Oh! give me back my Mountain Home. Quarte .25
Bird of Beauty. Song............ .25
I'm Leaving thee in Sorrow, Annie. Song...... .25
Ever of Thee. Song............ .25
Katie's Secret. Song............ .25
Grave of Rosabel. Song and Chorus........ .25
Three Roguish Chaps. Song............ .25
Scientific Frog. Song............ .25
Farewell! but we hope to meet again. Quartet. .25
Home of our Birth. Quartette............ .25
Day Dream. Solo and Chorus............ .25
When I am far away. Song............ .25
Farewell! I must leave thee. Ballad........ .30
Oh! if I were a Little Bird. Song........ .25
My Thoughts are of Thee. Ballad........ .25
Always Look on the Sunny Side. Ballad ...... .25
Dixey's Land. Song and Chorus........ .25
Happy Haidee. Song and Chorus........ .35
Bonnie, Bonnie Bell. Schottisch Ballad........ .25
Lovers' Parting. Song............ .25
Farmer Stubbs' Visit to New York City........ .35

Waltzes, Polkas, Schottishes, Marches, Rondos, Variations, and all kinds of Sheet Music published in America. Music published daily. All kinds of Musical Instruments and Music Merchandise at the lowest possible prices. Music sent by mail, post paid. A liberal discount to Schools, Teachers and Clergymen. The Trade supplied on the most liberal terms.

TESTIMONIALS of the HORACE WATERS PIANOS & MELODEONS

Having used one of the Horace Waters' Pianos in my family for three years, I am prepared to pronounce it *unequalled* in power, fulness and sweetness of tone, by any instrument which I have met with in the West.

Rev. Jas. W. Stewart, *Connersville, Ind.*

The Piano is just the one my wife and daughter desired. In tone it is richer, softer and sweeter than any I have heard for many years. There are many instruments in this place from different establishments, but it is conceded by the many who have heard it, and all who have played on it, that it is superior to any ever brought to this place. A number of ladies from other places have pronounced it one of the most delightful instruments to which they have ever listened. I must, in honesty, say that it is far better than I had hoped or expected to get.

Thos. W. F'y, *Crawfordsville, Ind.*

To the many flattering testimonials published, we feel bound to add another from ourselves. We have procured for one of our friends in this city, one of Waters' Pianos, and we can say that the instrument received is all that can be desired for elegance and quality.—*Pensacola Observer.*

If any of our friends want a number one Piano, at a reduced price, they can find it at the establishment of Horace Waters, 333 Broadway, New York. Jas. H. Moss, Esq., of this city, has had in use one of the Waters Pianos for over a year, and it has given great satisfaction, and it cost less than a similar instrument would in any establishment in the United States.—*Liberty (Missouri) Tribune.*

The Piano meets my expectations in every regard, that is, it is pronounced by musicians to be a good instrument.

Wm. H. Green, *Clinton, La.*

This is to certify that I have had one of the Horace Waters Pianos about four years, which has proved to be an excellent instrument, and grows better with use.

J. C. Wicker, *Yonkers, N. Y.*

Mr. Horace Waters—It is now more than two years since we received one of your Pianos. The instrument is admired by all, and has been highly commended by those who are good judges in such matters. For sweetness of tone we think it cannot be surpassed.

Mr. & Mrs. S. N. Robinson, *Whitneys Point, N. Y.*

Horace Waters, Esq.—The Piano you forwarded to my daughter is pronounced by those who claim to be judges a first-rate one. I like the tone very much myself, and my daughter is much gratified with the instrument, and pleased with it in every particular. This being the case, the "*rest of mankind*," and *womankind too,* should be content.

A. G. Hodges, *Covington, Ky.*

I am happy to say that the Piano I bought from you in November, 1856, has given me entire satisfaction, and is much admired both for its workmanship and melodeousness of tone. It seems to keep in tune well.

Wm'r Bicker, *Brooklyn, N. Y.*

Mr. Waters—*Dear Sir* : I received the Melodeon safe and in good order ; am well pleased with the external appearance, and the tone also.

Rev. Hiram Haynes, *Preston Hollow, N. Y.*

The Melodeon you sent me is in good order. I am now fully prepared to say that the instrument is *highly satisfactory.*

J. L. Smith, *Tioga, N. Y.*

The Melodeon has safely arrived. I feel obliged to you for your liberal discount.

Rev. J. M. McCormick, *Yaryesville, N. C.*

WAREROOMS, 333 BROADWAY, NEW YORK.